"*Speaking on Climate* [...] goes beyond speaking to the brain but speaking to the heart, body, and soul as the global artivism movement is urging us to do. It is a helpful and practical guide to communications that inspire and motivate action to respond to the climate crisis and importantly for anyone passionate about the state of our children and their children's futures."

—Kumi Naidoo, president of the Fossil Fuel Non-Proliferation Treaty Initiative

"Climate change? Sure, but don't limit yourself to that. This is a guide to impactful, even inspiring speechwriting no matter the cause. Rune's step-by-step thinking is the best-kept secret among first-rate speechwriters."

—Michael Long, coauthor of *The Molecule of More*

"*Speaking on Climate* by Rune Kier Nielsen is a crucial guide for anyone committed to using the power of words to drive meaningful climate action. As the founder of We Don't Have Time, the world's largest media platform for climate action, I have seen firsthand the importance of compelling, impactful communication. This book offers invaluable tools for crafting speeches that not only inform but inspire, moving hearts and minds towards urgent and effective change. A must-read for anyone who wants to speak up for our planet and make a real difference."

—Ingmar Rentzhog, founder & CEO, Wedonthavetime.org

"Rune's book has heart, humility and heaps of practical insight into how to create speeches that genuinely generate change. Highly recommended!"

—Simon Lancaster, speechwriter, TEDx talker, and author

"A genuine gem of a guide for speaking persuasively about the climate in public. . . . Climate rhetoric written in bold and searing letters."

—Mark Herron, PhD in rhetoric and author of *American Oratory— Powerful Speeches by the President and the People*

"This book is a stroke of genius for everybody interested in making an impact with their message, telling stories that hit the heart and inspiring change without scare tactics and doomsday talk. Rune Kier has really made a little masterpiece, and shares with us his many years of experience as an award-winning speechwriter for government ministers and leaders. . . . It is about how we use communication to create light in darkness, build bridges, and how we dare speak from the deep inside when we appeal to transformations."

    —Laura Storm, Regenerative Business & Leadership, Regenerators. co, WEF Young Global Leader, Greenbiz Worldchanger

"Knowledgeable and always inspiring Rune Kier Nielsen has written the most important book of the decade about how speech can create change."

    —Prins Marcus Valiant Lantz, rhetorical strategist and PhD

"Rune Kier Nielsen's *Speaking on Climate* inspires readers' passion for climate change and equips them with the tools to communicate effectively. Nielsen's expertise as a speechwriter guides readers to craft compelling and necessary dialogues that resonate deeply and inspire action. His practical insights and relatable examples make this book a must-read for those seeking to make a difference in the fight for climate change."

    —S. Kelley Harrell, author of *From Elder to Ancestor: Nature Kinship for All Seasons of Life*

"I think JFK, himself no mean speechmaker, would have loved this book: because as he said, 'The only reason to make a speech is to change the world.' In *Speaking on Climate*, Rune Kier Nielsen gives us a book to help save the world; and true to JFK he tells us the real purpose of a speech is not just to sound good, but to create change. UN climate advocate and award-winning speechwriter Rune Kier has written a guide to crafting a speech about the environment—or to making the environmental argument, whether you're speaking at a conference or rally."

    —Simon Gibson, CEO of World Speech Day

# SPEAKING ON CLIMATE

## A GUIDE TO SPEECHWRITING FOR A BETTER FUTURE

RUNE KIER NIELSEN

ZEST BOOKS
MINNEAPOLIS

TO MY WIFE, ANNA, AND MY CHILDREN, IDA AND
LUDVIG. THE LOVE I HOLD IN MY HEART FOR YOU AND MY
CONCERN FOR YOUR FUTURE DROVE AN IDEA IN MY HEAD
TO BECOME THE BOOK YOU NOW HOLD IN YOUR HANDS.
I HOPE IT WILL HELP YOU AND OTHERS DEFEND OUR
WORLD'S BALANCE AND CREATE A BETTER FUTURE—
THE FUTURE WE ALL DESERVE.

Text copyright © 2025 by Rune Kier Nielsen

All rights reserved. No part of this book may be reproduced, stored in a retrieval system, or transmitted in any form or by any means—electronic, mechanical, photocopying, recording, or otherwise—without the prior written permission of Lerner Publishing Group, Inc., except for the inclusion of brief quotations in an acknowledged review.

Zest Books™
An imprint of Lerner Publishing Group, Inc.
241 First Avenue North
Minneapolis, MN 55401 USA

For reading levels and more information, look up this title at www.lernerbooks.com.
Visit us at zestbooks.net.

Designed by Kimberly Morales

Main body text set in Adobe Caslon Pro.
Typeface provided by Adobe Systems.

**Library of Congress Cataloging-in-Publication Data**

Names: Kier Nielsen, Rune, author.
Title: Speaking on climate: a guide to speechwriting for a better future / Rune Kier Nielsen.
Description: Minneapolis: Zest Books, [2025] | Includes bibliographical references and index. | Audience: Ages 11–18. | Audience: Grades 7–9. | Summary: "What makes a speech well written, memorable, and effective? And how can someone apply those skills to climate justice? Former UN Public Advocacy Lead on Climate Action and award-winning speechwriter Rune Kier Nielsen will answer these questions and more in this timely guide"—Provided by publisher.
Identifiers: LCCN 2024023482 (print) | LCCN 2024023483 (ebook) | ISBN 9798765627570 (library binding) | ISBN 9798765627587 (paperback) | ISBN 9798765659656 (epub)
Subjects: LCSH: Climatic changes—Juvenile literature. | Speechwriting—Juvenile literature. | Public speaking—Juvenile literature.
Classification: LCC QC903.15 .K534 2025 (print) | LCC QC903.15 (ebook) | DDC 808.06/9—dc23/eng/20240715

LC record available at https://lccn.loc.gov/2024023482
LC ebook record available at https://lccn.loc.gov/2024023483

Manufactured in The United States of America
1-1010944-52138-11/22/2024

# TABLE OF CONTENTS

**INTRODUCTION** .................................. 7

**CHAPTER 1**
STAND BY YOUR EMOTIONS .................. 25

**CHAPTER 2**
BE TRUE TO YOUR WORLDVIEW ............ 41

**CHAPTER 3**
FIND INSPIRATION IN THE PAST ............ 61

**CHAPTER 4**
BUILD A GOLDEN BRIDGE .................... 81

**CHAPTER 5**
TELL THE STORY OF YOUR JOURNEY .......... 95

**CHAPTER 6**
CREATE COMMITMENT FOR CHANGE ........ 107

**CHAPTER 7**
USE THE ONE RING ........................... 121

**CHAPTER 8**
THE SOUND OF A LEADER ................... 137

**CHAPTER 9**
MAKE YOUR MESSAGE TRAVEL .............. 149

**AFTERWORD** .................................. 163

**SOURCE NOTES** ............................... 173

**SELECTED BIBLIOGRAPHY** ................... 185

**FURTHER INFORMATION** ..................... 188

**INDEX** ......................................... 196

# INTRODUCTION

In 2013 I was the speechwriter in the Ministry for Climate, Energy and Buildings in the Danish government. I was tasked with writing a speech for the minister who would be opening an international medical conference on birth control and sexual health in Copenhagen, Denmark.

Most speeches written in government or the corporate world get very little personal attention from high-ranking speakers and will often turn out as more generic scripts. This speech, however, was written under the ideal circumstances. It had the focused attention of the minister in charge of climate policy in the Danish government, who had decided to attend because his brother—the event organizer—had invited him, and because other speakers included the Danish royal family. Where many speeches to senior leadership go through numerous approvals and extensive—often conflicting—corrections, this speech did not.

The speech was built around the story of a fictitious woman, Sarah, and the health challenges she endured during a pregnancy in a world ravaged by climate change. Sarah's story was supported with facts and scenarios for the future. The end had *tricolon* (rule of three) with *anaphora* (start repetition)—aimed to get applause. It had self-deprecating humor to make the speaker more relatable and clear calls to action to have a lasting impact.

On paper, it was a good speech. The manuscript won two Cicero Speechwriting Awards—the Oscars of speechwriting—in the categories of Government and Environment/Energy/

Sustainability. David Murray, the CEO of Pro Rhetoric and Professional Speechwriters Association (PSA) and a judge of the Cicero Speechwriting Awards, wrote, "By understanding the plight of Sarah, we understand the plight of all humanity—and we see the chance to change Sarah's destiny, and our own."

Another Cicero judge, political speechwriter Tom Rosshirt, wrote, "Wow. I've been listening to climate change arguments since I first wrote a speech on the topic for Al Gore in 1997. This is the first time I've heard it put this way—and it is arresting."

But in practice, the speech did not live up to my or the judges' expectations. Right before the speech was given, the Danish crown princess Mary spoke about a real girl she met named Palmyra. That took some of the air out of the fictional story of Sarah. When it was the minister's turn to deliver the speech I had written, he improvised a section on basic utility prices in the twentieth century. The biggest applause he received was when he self-deprecatingly corrected himself for misspeaking a minor fact. The speech was far less impressive than I had intended, and the audience seemed to agree. I still hoped that it had made an impact.

Seven years after he gave that speech, as COVID-19 hit the world, I contacted eight people from the conference and asked about their impressions of the speech. Three did not remember it, one had not heard it for sure, and one did not have time to answer. Three people *did* remember the speech. Yet what they remembered seemed to have nothing to do with the impact of the speech itself. They had signed up for a conference on pregnancy prevention, reproduction, and sexual health, not climate. So they remembered Palmyra's story because it was about the right to birth control and family planning, whereas Sarah's story was about climate change. And they all claimed not to have learned anything new—only confirmation of what they already knew.

Ideal conditions made for an award-winning speech on paper,

but change did not happen. The speech "Climate Change and the Story of Sarah" did not change the world.

This, I realized, had nothing to do with how it was performed. My goal had been to write a *good* speech, but to mobilize the audience, I needed to have written a *do-good* speech: one that inspires its audience to act. The mistake was mine alone as the speechwriter because I did not think about the long-term lifespan of the speech.

I have since learned the skills and tools to create a speech that has a lasting impact. By studying the great speeches that inspired change throughout history, learning from experts, and analyzing and adjusting my own speeches, I identified patterns that I have consolidated into nine recommendations for making impactful speeches—for speaking on climate. The nine chapters in this book each elaborate on one of those suggestions, providing examples of both good and bad speeches and giving guidance on what to do (or not to do) when writing your own. It's just as important to study unsuccessful speeches as successful ones as often we know neither the intended nor the actual effect of a speech but rather have access only to some evaluation of it years past its delivery. After reading this book, you will understand what I have come to learn about speechwriting. Let my mistakes inform your success. Then we can do better together.

I firmly believe that a speech has far greater potential than merely *being* good—it can *do* good. It can motivate people to take real-life action, move us from individual pursuits to collective impact, create a shared sense of community, and even change people's lives by enabling them to tell their own stories in a new way. A do-good speech is so much more than empty words. For those in the audience, your speech can change their world, and what follows can do even more. That is your power.

We are facing enormous challenges with the climate crisis

and biodiversity loss. These challenges demand all hands on deck. People from all disciplines and sectors have an obligation to contribute with their competences, including speechwriters. I have written this book for those of you who want to speak out on climate, environment, or biodiversity. You, who want to use your speech to create change. You, who want to strengthen support for climate action through your words. When you are preparing to speak about climate, many choices have already been made. You know what the speech will be about, you know that people will likely show up because they are interested, and you know that you will likely share certain values with the audience. You also know that the audience has already acted on their values by showing up. They are primed for action.

The climate movement is about hope. Many of us feel hopeless when leaders take insufficient action. Is there hope for the climate? How might we change the world fast enough to avoid the worst consequences of global warming? How can I do my part? Those are some of the questions your audience might struggle with, making them unsure how to act to make a difference.

Your speech will have to provide answers that inspire hope, leading your audience to take action. Because the world needs action. When you speak to a crowd, you have to choose if you want your words to push people away, to be quickly forgotten, or to receive applause. If the goal is to make a difference, you need something more. You need to use the speech as a catalyst for reflection, dialogue, and action afterward. We have all heard too many ineffective speeches about climate. Let us start writing ones that work.

W. E. B. Du Bois was highly influential in the foundation of contemporary sociology. He was an activist and cofounder of the National Association for the Advancement of Colored People (NAACP) and a consultant at the founding of the United Nations after World War II (1939–1945). He said, "Now is the accepted time, not tomorrow, not some more convenient season. It is today that our best work can be done and not some future day or future year. It is today that we fit ourselves for the greater usefulness of tomorrow. Today is the seed time, now are the hours of work, and tomorrow comes the harvest and the playtime."

After reading this book, I hope that you will be able to act according to your beliefs using the power of words to change the world for the better.

## A QUICK DIVE INTO RHETORIC

This book is a "seed" to help you achieve greater usefulness, and together we can harvest what grows from it. To do that, we must first take a quick dive into the history of rhetoric.

Humans had always spoken, rallied, and told stories around the campfire, but it is with the emergence of democracy in ancient Greece some twenty-five hundred years ago that the art of rhetoric and persuasion as we know it first began to take form. Aristotle led this change. For twenty years, he studied in the academy of one of the all-time most influential Greek philosophers, Plato. During that time, Aristotle moved away from philosophy to a more observational, and empirical approach to leadership—a more useful method, adaptable, multidisciplinary, and relevant for participating in Greek society. Eventually, leading Greek philosophers relocated to Rome, where they inspired a new generation of rhetoricians (people who study and use the science of rhetoric).

*Rhetoric*, a collection of Aristotle's teachings, has been and still is compulsory reading at universities across the world. Through this book, two millennia's worth of aristocrats, politicians, and students have learned about the components of rhetoric. Aristotle introduces readers to the three modes of persuasion:

- Ethos appeals to the character of the speaker by demonstrating trustworthiness and goodwill.
- Pathos appeals to the emotions and values of the audience to engage them and motivate them to action.
- Logos appeals to reason and logic by presenting arguments that are coherent, rational, and supported by evidence to persuade the audience intellectually or at least justify their preexisting attitudes and actions.

After that, Aristotle outlines the five canons of rhetoric, a series of steps to produce an argument. They are *inventio* (generating ideas, arguments, and evidence), *dispositio* (structuring the speech for clarity, coherence, and effectiveness), *elocutio* (choice of language,

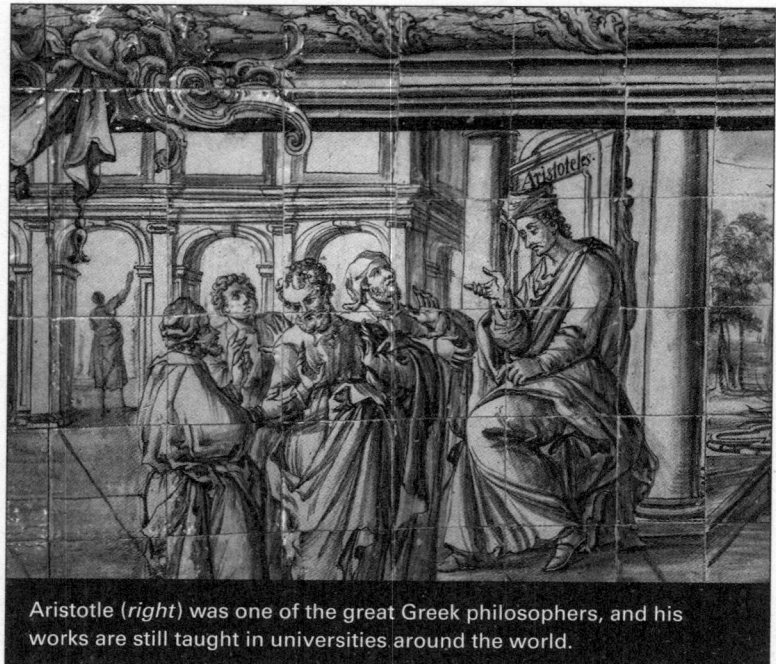

Aristotle (*right*) was one of the great Greek philosophers, and his works are still taught in universities around the world.

tone, and stylistic devices), *memoria* (memory techniques to remember the key components), and *pronuntiatio* (performance of the speech with voice, gestures, and style).

Finally, he describes three types of persuasive speech. The first is *demonstrative*, or *epideictic, rhetoric*—using praise or blame to reinforce or challenge existing values and beliefs in the present moment. *Forensic* or *judicial rhetoric* establishes facts or judgments about the past. And *deliberative* or *political rhetoric* is used to persuade an audience to make decisions or take action that affects the future.

In this book we attempt to balance ethos, pathos, and logos in a process of invention, arrangement, and style in the deliberative mode of persuasion. That is what most of us will use when speaking up for climate—and it is also what other historical figures have used to argue their case for change. One such figure was Alexander the Great, one of Aristotle's pupils. When he became the sole king of Macedonia in 336 BCE, he used Aristotle's techniques to inspire his army for conquest, to engage in diplomatic relations with other nations, and to conduct matters of state.

From Macedonia, Alexander conquered all the way to present-day Pakistan and parts of India, and he became a pharaoh in Egypt. In ten years, he had created one of the largest empires in history. He is widely considered as one of the greatest military strategists of all time. Much of his fame rests on his ability to inspire his soldiers. But it didn't last forever. Alexander wanted to cross what is now called the Beas River close to modern-day Jalandhar, Punjab, India. But his soldiers wanted to go home. They feared the superior strength of the Persian army with war elephants and archers crossing the river. And so, Alexander turned to the rhetorical tools Aristotle had taught him. He gave a speech. His task was to motivate the tired soldiers to cross the river and fight unknown enemies far from home.

It did not work. But Alexander spoke the best he could,

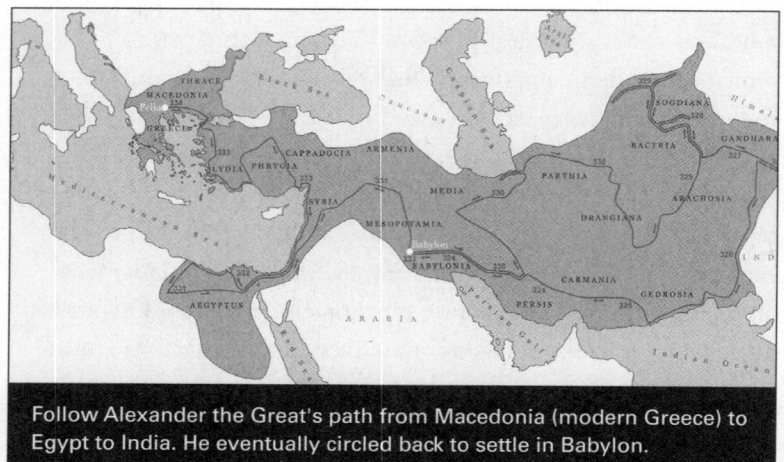

Follow Alexander the Great's path from Macedonia (modern Greece) to Egypt to India. He eventually circled back to settle in Babylon.

and I will go through that speech in chapter 8. A few years after Alexander returned home, he died in Babylon. Many historians argue that Alexander's leadership and rhetoric kept an empire together—in any case, it fell apart soon after his death.

As a consequence, Aristotle had to flee Athens for exile on the island Euboea. Here he gathered his lecture notes in a book, and that is what became known as *Rhetoric*. He also wrote books called *Poetics* and *Politics*. Metaphors—rhetorical devices used to better understand something by describing it as something else and thus highlighting different characteristics—are mentioned in both *Rhetoric* and *Poetics*. In *Rhetoric*, Aristotle writes that metaphors cannot be used to define or understand something, yet he uses them throughout the book to help the reader along. In *Poetics*, he writes that the good use of metaphors is that they demonstrate the similarity in what we perceive as difference. That means that metaphors have the power to change how we see things by making them similar to something we know. It is much like how storytelling has the potential to change our perspective on the world through identification. Identification works by simultaneously highlighting a shared characteristic and using it as an invitation for your audience to see the world as you see it. In *Rhetoric*, Aristotle writes, "Now strange words simply puzzle us; ordinary words convey only what we know already; it is from metaphor that we can best get ahold of something fresh."

Many years after Aristotle's death, in 80 BCE a young Roman man named Sextus Roscius was arrested and accused of killing his father. Patricide was serious. The penalty was death. Sextus hired Marcus Tullius Cicero to defend him. Cicero had studied classical rhetoric and Greek philosophy at an academy in Rome. It was Cicero's first trial, at twenty-six years old, and it became a trial by metaphor. The prosecutors wanted to convict Sextus. They attempted to make him appear guilty and nonhuman to the jury, likening him to a dog that one would kill if it hurt its master. But Cicero used the metaphor to his advantage and made the case that a dog does not kill its father, and so patricide was out of the question. Then he turned the metaphor on its head to argue that it was the prosecutors who were dogs because they wanted to convict an innocent man for money.

Cicero exposed the prosecutors' circular argument: Sextus was a dog, and therefore he killed his father, which proved that he was a dog in the first place. Then Cicero addressed the jury. He appealed to their emotions and humanity. They were not dogs but human, and they could prove it by freeing Sextus in the name of morality, mercy, and justice.

Cicero won the case for Sextus, and eventually, he became a prominent citizen of Rome, writing several books and treatises on rhetoric. One of them is *De Oratore* (on the orator), which discusses the ideal speaker and the art of rhetoric as a conversation drawing on Greek rhetorical theories and Cicero's own ideas and experiences as a prominent Roman political leader and orator. In the same ambivalent style as Aristotle, he criticized the unethical use of metaphors—through a metaphor. He compared metaphors for clothes intended to keep people warm being used now for decorations and aesthetics. His book became another staple for university reading lists across the world.

Cicero rose in reputation and became consul. But he fell from grace when he attacked Roman emperor Mark Antony in a series of speeches. He was added to a list of enemies of the state with a bounty on his head. His mistake was being on the wrong side of a battle for the leader of the Roman Republic. But it did not help that he had used metaphors to compare Mark Antony to sheep and dogs. He was executed, and his severed head and right hand were displayed as trophies on the rostrum in the Roman Forum as a warning. The rostrum had been a platform for some of Cicero's most stirring speeches.

## A CLIMATE FLASHBACK

With a bit of background on rhetoric and persuasion, you will more easily see the successes and failures of climate communication in our modern world. For instance, you can say that humans have always been part of nature, the environment, and changing climates. Drought, floods, ice ages, and deserts have set the stage for our evolution and development, and we have affected our environment in turn. Human beings in Australia forty-five thousand years ago and in America ten thousand years ago caused several large animal species to go extinct. And ten thousand years ago African farming practices likely increased the size of the Saharan desert. But since then, a change has happened. A change in scale. We are living in what many scientists call the Anthropocene epoch, where humans are the dominant force shaping nature—and we have to take responsibility for how we shape it.

Scientists have long known and warned against the

mechanisms behind our present climate crisis. In 1896 Swedish Nobel Prize winner Svante Arrhenius wrote about coal emitting carbon dioxide ($CO_2$) and leading to global warming. In 1958 an observatory in Hawaii issued the first scientific warning about high concentrations of $CO_2$ in the atmosphere. Meanwhile, scientists working for major oil companies were already making an accurate prognosis of the consequences from emitting $CO_2$.

After the assassination of US president John F. Kennedy in 1963, his vice president, Lyndon B. Johnson, took office. In a speech to Congress two years later, Johnson became the first US president to mention global warming as a political problem, stating, "This generation has altered the composition of the atmosphere on a global scale through radioactive materials and a steady increase in carbon dioxide from the burning of fossil fuels."

In 1975 geophysicist Wallace S. Broecker penned an article titled "Climatic Change: Are We on the Brink of a Pronounced Global Warming?" Free market economist Milton Friedman and his wife, Rose Friedman, wrote the bestseller *Free to Choose* in 1979, where he called climate and pollution "market flaws" and argued for a climate tax: "If we want to have the electricity with less pollution, we shall have to pay, directly or indirectly, a high enough price for the electricity to cover the extra costs."

Friedman served as an economic adviser to Ronald Reagan in the United States and to Margaret Thatcher in the United Kingdom. His role advising leaders in two different countries signaled broad political support for climate action. That support was relevant when Norwegian prime minister Gro Harlem Brundtland was put in charge of a report in 1983 on the state of Earth's climate for the General Assembly of the United Nations (UN) in 1987. It was called *Our Common Future*, but most people know it as the Brundtland Report, and it launched the concept of "sustainable development" and increased the awareness of global warming. Just two years later, in 1989, Margaret Thatcher was the prime minister in the United Kingdom and gave a speech at the UN General Assembly, singling out the climate crisis: "Of all the challenges faced by the world community in those four years [since her last speech], one has grown clearer than any other in both urgency and importance—I refer to the threat to our global environment. I shall take the opportunity of addressing the general assembly to speak on that subject alone."

Thatcher encouraged humans to live with nature and not dominate it. Invoking the Bible, she reminded the audience that humans are not the Lord, but part of the Lord's creation, shepherds of the planet tasked with preserving life along with all its mystery and wonder. She also urged the creation of a framework for global climate action at the Earth Summit in Rio de Janeiro, Brazil, three years later. That is what became the United Nations Framework Convention on Climate Change (UNFCCC) and the Conference of the Parties (COP) process. These parties are countries that have signed a treaty—for example, the Paris

Margaret Thatcher addressed the UN General Assembly at the UN headquarters in New York on November 8, 1989.

Agreement, an international agreement to address climate change. It is usually called the Climate COP to differentiate it from other Conferences of the Parties aimed at other subjects. UN Climate COPs are annual global meetings where countries collaborate to set goals, make plans, and track progress on combating issues such as climate change, while also addressing funding and adaptation strategies.

At that Earth Summit in Rio de Janeiro, one speaker grasped the attention of the world. It was twelve-year-old Severn Cullis-Suzuki: "Coming up here today, I have no hidden agenda. I am fighting for my future. Losing my future is not like losing an election, or a few points on the stock market. I am here to speak for all generations to come. I am here to speak—speak on behalf of the starving children around the world whose cries go unheard. I am here to speak for the countless animals dying across this planet, because they have nowhere left to go."

She was angry and not afraid to show it. "In my anger, I'm not blind; and in my fear, I'm not afraid of telling the world how I feel." And Severn wasn't afraid of pointing fingers and attributing blame: "Do not forget why you are attending these conferences—who you're doing this for. We are your own children. You are deciding what kind of a world we are growing up in. Parents should be able to comfort their children by saying, 'Everything's going to be all right; it's not the end of the world, and we're . . . and we're doing the best we can.' But I don't think you can say that to us anymore. Are we even on your list of priorities?"

The Earth Summit embraced the Brundtland Report and the concept of sustainable development. In 1997 the Kyoto Protocol was formed to put a price on carbon aligned with what Milton Friedman has proposed previously. Things appeared to be in motion. The world had been summoned, and anticipation was through the roof. But despite these steps, little changed. Emissions

Severn Cullis-Suzuki (*right*) gives a speech at a Climate Strike event in Vancouver, Canada, alongside Greta Thunberg (*center*) and other climate activists in October 2019.

continued to climb. The Kyoto Protocol did not go into effect until 2005, and it seemed the pendulum of public opinion swung the other way.

At the same time, governments around the world were beginning to acknowledge global warming. Yet major oil companies had known for quite some time. At first, they were exploring the consequences of fossil fuels emitting $CO_2$, then they were warning decision-makers of the effects, and then they changed strategy entirely from research to flat-out denial of human-caused global warming and the negative effect of fossil fuels emitting $CO_2$. They developed a propaganda strategy aimed at sowing doubt and actively opposing political regulation by focusing on the uncertainty of the scientific consensus on global warming. This was extremely effective at stalling much-needed climate action around the world, but especially in the United States, which was a major economic power whose lack of action had global consequences.

During the 1992 Earth Summit, Gore published the book *Earth in the Balance: Ecology and the Human Spirit* proposing a "Global Marshall Plan" for climate. It did not reach very far. But after he lost the presidential election to George W. Bush in 2000, he made a dent in the public perception. His presentation *An Inconvenient Truth* popularized his concept of a climate crisis and moral responsibility. Climatewise, the election was between Gore's concept of a "climate crisis" and Bush's framing as "climate change." In 2006 Gore's presentation was made into a documentary, and it won an Oscar for Best Documentary the following year. In his acceptance speech, Gore said, "People all over the world. We need to solve the climate crisis. It is not a political issue; it is a moral issue. We have everything we need to get started with the possible exception of the will to act. That is a renewable resource—let's renew it." Later, in 2007, he won a Nobel Peace Prize along with the UN IPCC and established the Climate Reality Project in 2011.

The presidential election in 2008 saw Bush hand over the White House to Barack Obama. Obama had a more progressive approach to climate, yet still used the term "climate change." For numerous reasons little was done, and the promise of the COP15 negotiations in Copenhagen in 2009 ended without a legally binding treaty and only with vague declarations of intent.

The devastating disappointment of COP15 changed the game. It left many activists and protesters disillusioned. It led some, including me, to make climate their battle. And it shifted the focus from persuasion by science to combat by communication. This shift was described by the European Climate Foundation—the aim would no longer be to convince everybody that climate was the most important issue. Now the aim would be to insert climate as central regardless of the issue.

As the Danish government minister for climate and energy

leading up to COP15, Connie Hedegaard was in charge of COP15 in Copenhagen, Denmark. But she was appointed as the European Commission's commissioner for climate just before the event. In 2012 she launched the climate campaign: "A World You Like." It signaled a change in addressing the climate crisis as a single issue to highlight how the climate crisis affects other issues including the economy, the environment, and our health and daily life.

The UNFCCC negotiated the Paris Agreement, and it was signed in December 2015 with massive backing for clear targets to prevent the rise of average global temperatures from exceeding 2°C (3.6°F), and aim for below 1.5°C (2.7°F). This was to keep the world from crossing various tipping points that would further accelerate emissions and push the climate crisis out of human control.

Tipping points are "critical thresholds beyond which a system reorganizes, often abruptly and/or irreversibly," according to the Intergovernmental Panel on Climate Change (IPCC). One example of a tipping point is forests. Through photosynthesis, trees capture carbon from the air and help reduce $CO_2$ in the atmosphere. Yet global warming is increasing wildfires, which burn more trees, thus emitting $CO_2$ into the atmosphere and increasing global warming even further. A small change can create a tipping point leading to massive escalating change.

But the pendulum swung again. In 2016 Donald Trump won the White House on a platform of climate denial, conspiracy theory, and the belief that the climate crisis was a Chinese hoax designed to hurt US trade. Trump pulled the United States out of the Paris Agreement. Luckily, another type of tipping point had occurred, and Trump was unable to stop climate measures in companies and governments across the world. Renewable energy had become cheaper than fossil fuels in many cases.

Joe Biden took over the White House in 2020, and in his speech for nomination to be the candidate, he spoke of climate change as "an existential threat." After the election, he expanded on the climate crisis as one of a list of the "battles of our time." He said, "Climate change will continue to threaten the lives and livelihoods, and public health and economics of our existence and, literally, the very existence of our planet."

And in his inauguration speech in January 2021, Biden said, "A cry for survival comes from the planet itself. A cry that can't be any more desperate or any more clear."

In the late summer of 2023, the United Nations held a Climate Ambition Summit. UN secretary general António Guterres said, "Humanity has opened the gates of hell."

A desperate cry, a battle of our age, and the gates of hell are only the most recent words used in a long history of speaking about climate action. What words will be yours?

# CHAPTER 1
# STAND BY YOUR EMOTIONS

Does the idea of giving a speech in front of an audience terrify you? Many people experience anxiety about public speaking. It can be frightening to have everyone's eyes and ears on you. You might feel vulnerable taking a stand on an important issue or fear that your words will be weighed and judged. And you might be afraid that your emotions will undermine the very message that causes those emotions. If your audience sees that you're emotional, won't they dismiss everything you say?

On the contrary, emotions have a lot to do with persuasion. Because most of us—if not all—know what it's like to be nervous, we can identify with the fear of public speaking. I have come to understand that any nervousness you feel will create a bond between you and your audience. Taking a little time to breathe or tripping over your words shows the audience that you are human, that you are just like them and, perhaps most crucially, that your message matters to you. What you have to say must be important or else you would not take the stand when you are this nervous. In this way, you are already one step ahead in making them care about your message.

Emotions make your message matter, so you shouldn't hide them. They are contagious. Your best emotional argument is your truth—you just have to find the words that express it. If you are angry about the lack of climate action, you want the audience to share your anger and frustration. If you are hopeful that certain actions will make a difference, you want the audience to share that same hope. If you believe we are in desperate need of adequate climate action, you want the audience to share that feeling of urgency.

You must practice your speech, of course, but there is no need to be afraid of your emotions; they help you. Your emotions are your superpower. Unfortunately, many do not see it that way—and there is reason for that.

## EMOTIONS ARE PERSUASIVE

It is a common misunderstanding that we should never show emotion and that the subjects we talk about should always be conveyed in an objective and neutral manner to be credible and convincing. These misconceptions have been proven to be plain wrong—again and again. In his book *How to Fight Inequality: (And Why That Fight Needs You)*, Ben Phillips argues that simply relaying scientific facts and data is not enough to inspire action or drive change as research has shown that factual information alone often fails to resonate with people or motivate them to engage with complex social issues. He emphasizes the importance of framing messages in ways that connect emotionally and personally with audiences by focusing on relatable narratives and human stories.

These misconceptions are remnants from the Age of Enlightenment, an intellectual and philosophical movement from seventeenth- and eighteenth-century Europe that emphasized rationality, empiricism, and liberal values. The Enlightenment, also called the Age of Reason, is said to have started either when philosopher René Descartes declared "Cogito, ergo sum" (I think, therefore I am) in 1644 or when Isaac Newton discovered the laws of gravity in 1687. The Enlightenment slowly came to dominate Western thought. In Europe during the 1600s, many still saw the

Isaac Newton studied Aristotle's and other philosophers' work before he turned to the scientific method.

world as chaotic and full of unknown forces, and education was only accessible to royalty, privileged laypersons, or people pursuing a life within the church. But after English philosopher Francis Bacon pioneered the empirical scientific method, people started to see the world as structured and orderly. Enlightenment thinkers believed it was only a matter of time before we would understand the world and the laws that govern it by using the scientific method and logic.

This age has had a major influence on our understanding of climate and environment. Following the scientific method to conduct experiments, people discovered the role of water pollution in spreading diseases such as cholera and how to use steam to power engines. The same science that sought to overcome suffering set a standard for empirical experiments and created the foundation for industrialization, which increased the use of fossil fuels and the emission of greenhouse gases including $CO_2$.

The paradoxes of the Enlightenment do not stop there. Its ideals of liberty, equality, and progress contended with the monarchies that had ruled Europe for centuries, leading to the establishment of the system of democracy that enables us to vote for climate action. But progress has become synonymous with economic opportunity, and the governments that emerged out of the Enlightenment sought constant economic growth. That growth is contributing to rising greenhouse gas emissions.

The Enlightenment created the problem and the solution. By developing scientific experiments, Enlightenment thinkers had found a method that any other scientist could use to gain knowledge. They believed that people would always act in their own self-interest, and if everyone had the same facts, they would make the same decisions on the basis of rational thought. This would unify people and reduce inequality. But over time, these ideas reduced to "more needs more" and "I need more." The pursuit of happiness and freedom for all became the freedom to pursue your own individual happiness—often at the expense of the environment, climate, and other people.

If the Enlightenment ideals of objectivity and rational argument were all we needed to convince people that the climate crisis is real and that we need to act now, then things would be very different. Climate scientists have tried for decades to communicate the urgency of the problem with graphs, averages, and predictions drawn from their scientific research. Yet this has resulted in little progress.

Using scientific concepts to make an argument is one example of logos. Science is useful, of course; it tells us what is happening in the world around us, what to expect based on those conditions, and what we might be able to change by adjusting different factors. But science does not tell us *why* we must change our ways (pathos), and it does not instill in us a belief that it is possible and necessary to change (ethos). That science alone is insufficient to persuade people should be no surprise, as successful rhetoric has required a balance of ethos, pathos, and logos since the time of Aristotle.

Taking concepts directly from science can actually kill the audience's emotions and undermine your efforts to persuade them. Evoking scientific concepts risks alienating your audience if they don't possess the same knowledge as you, and as a consequence, the crowd might only hear jargon and drift off or misunderstand your point. It's important to meet your audience where they're at by focusing on what matters to them without getting too abstract.

Here are some words that I would recommend you avoid when making an emotional case to people who might disagree with you. Be mindful, though, that the understanding of certain words does change, although changing it is hard and takes a long time.

- "Global warming" or "climate change" are concepts taken directly from scientific research papers. Yet they do not convey the seriousness or urgency of the climate crisis, and they might sound like a pleasant trip south for a vacation getaway. When searching for a term that fits your emotional approach, consider *climate crisis*, *climate breakdown*, *climate apocalypse*, *climate cliff*, *global boiling*, *global overheating*, or *global weirding*. Each of these communicates an emotion more strongly than "warming" or "change."

- "Sustainability" and "sustainable development" are becoming commonplace but mostly in the climate sphere. They are not bad terms, but very few people understand the details behind them, and they have become feel-good buzzwords that elicit very few emotions. Often, you are better off talking about something being cleaner, safer, or healthier.

- "Net-zero" or "carbon-neutral" produce more obstacles than connections for your audience. Nobody wants to aim for nothing or stay neutral. We all want to move ahead and do things better. Like "sustainability," net-zero has become a corporate and policy buzzword that says very little to most people.

- "Mitigation," "adaptation," and "resilience" are all heavily used concepts in climate jargon but also heavily misunderstood outside of it. "Mitigation" leads people to think of mediating conflicts, and some know it as a legal term with negative connotations. "Adaptation" is often understood as adjusting to a new situation or even the adaptation of a book into a movie. Your point will be clearer if you talk about how we make changes so we can live with the impacts of the climate crisis.

- *Carbon, carbon, carbon.* This term appears everywhere in climate rhetoric: carbon footprint, carbon budget, carbon dioxide, $CO_2$, $CO_2e$, carbon removal, carbon sinks, carbon capture, and other chemical abbreviations. Yet some people know carbon as simply one of many elements necessary for life—or something used in the construction of bicycles for professional racing. It's unlikely that chemistry will make your audience emotional.

We can see the contradiction between Enlightenment ideals and Aristotle's concepts at play by looking at US politics. From the perspective of the Enlightenment, we would all vote according to our economic interests. Yet many working-class Americans vote for Republicans promising tax cuts to the wealthy at their own expense. And similarly, many people vote for Democrats with climate policies that will not benefit themselves but the next generation. In either case, voters are not acting out of short-term self-interest. And that is both good and bad news. The reasons for voting for and against pro-climate measures are the same. The conclusion is that we do not need to change or overcome most people's values and emotions— we only need to connect their values to climate action. We need to argue why the values people already have should lead them to climate action. If we do this right, short-term self-interest wouldn't present an obstacle. We can even persuade people to vote in favor of expensive solutions. We can and should speak about values and principles—and emotions.

So how do we do it?

## DON'T SHY AWAY FROM EMOTION

A major reason that we are still not progressing fast enough toward solving the climate crisis is that too many people talk about the crisis and all its doomsday scenarios in a monotone voice and without any change in pulse. Without emotions. Without urgency. The format has to fit the content. We can see the proof for ourselves: the greatest climate movement the world has ever seen was mobilized by the clear, relatable emotions of Swedish teenager Greta Thunberg—not the rational presentations of graphs and averages from scientists.

In 2019 Thunberg took the stage at the UN Climate Action Summit and, on behalf of youth everywhere, spoke thunder to world leaders, scorning them for inaction on climate. Here is the start of her speech:

> My message is that we'll be watching you.
>
> This is all wrong. I shouldn't be up here. I should be back in school on the other side of the ocean. Yet you all come to us young people for hope. How dare you!
>
> You have stolen my dreams and my childhood with your empty words. And yet I'm one of the lucky ones. People are suffering. People are dying. Entire ecosystems are collapsing. We are in the beginning of a mass extinction, and all you can talk about is money and fairy tales of eternal economic growth. How dare you!

The speech demonstrates that Thunberg knows the science. But her mission is not to tell people about that science, her mission

Greta Thunberg's anger shows on her face and in her words at the UN Climate Action Summit in 2019.

is to show the audience what to feel about the facts they hear. She uses science as a foundation that everyone should already know and agree on. From there, she draws her conclusion about the world leaders who aren't doing enough about climate change: Either they are evil, or they do not listen. She does not provide a thorough summary of the science; instead, she tells people how to feel about the work they do (or fail to do), and she uses words that match her emotions. The format fits the content.

Let's look at another example. Once when tasked with writing a speech about climate for an audience of adult decision-makers, I had grown tired of all the science of the climate debate. The numbers, the percentages, the averages, the medians, the abbreviations—it was too much. So, I changed directions and wrote a speech about a penguin to appeal to their protective instincts. It goes like this:

> Emperor penguins always return to the same spot of ice year after year. They can't climb so the ice must be flat ocean ice. Here they mate and lay their eggs. One couple, one egg. The same couple every year and every year a new egg—but just one. A mommy, a daddy, and an egg or a chick. That is the nuclear penguin family.
>
> When she has laid her egg, the mommy returns to the ocean one hundred miles [161 km] away to eat and gather strength after the pregnancy and the egg-laying. Daddy stays with the egg until the chick hatches about seventy days after.
>
> At this point he has been without food or drink for almost four months, standing on the same patch of ice and balancing the egg on his feet. His one task is keeping the egg warm with his body heat. It is not easy being a penguin dad. He will lose half his body weight while waiting in the absolute coldest temperatures on planet Earth—through snowstorms of a severity not seen outside Antarctica. But he waits. He waits for the egg to hatch so that he may see his baby chick, and he waits for his mate to come back. They are a couple, and they stick together.
>
> He has done it before, and he looks forward to the first cracks in the egg. When the little one is out, he must take care of it. A baby penguin is too small and fragile to even touch the cold ice. Daddy must wait with the chick standing on his feet until the mother comes back from the ocean. Otherwise, the chick will freeze to death.
>
> They are completely dependent on each other. If daddy leaves the baby before mommy arrives, the baby will

die of hunger or cold. If mommy is too late, daddy can't make it to the ocean in time and he will die of hunger. It is a tricky balance on the ice. And it does not always work out. There are many challenges.

Our daddy has been standing on the ice for close to four months now. No food, no water, and an egg balancing on his feet the whole time. He is growing impatient and hungry. Time is coming. He hears a crack and looks down in anticipation. But it is not a crack in the egg. The sound comes from below. The great ocean ice sheet below the entire penguin colony is breaking up. The smaller ice sheets are tumbling and turning with the change in balance and ocean current. He loses his balance, and the

These emperor penguins survived the frigid winter and now must care for their hatching chicks.

egg rolls from his feet—towards the edge of the ice sheet.

If the egg is on the ice for too long it will freeze, and the baby will die. But the daddy can't pick it up. He can only follow alongside the egg as it rolls across the ice and falls from the edge into the water. He can only dive in and swim next to it as it descends towards the ocean floor.

He dives for twenty minutes and feels the lactic acid pumping through his body. He must surface to breathe again. So, he leaves the egg behind—an egg he has balanced on his feet and kept warm for four months—and he turns his eyes upward. Here he sees all the other penguin daddies. All the eggs from the colony have tumbled into the water and the daddies are maniacally diving after them in the water. A whole generation of emperor penguins has been lost in an instant.

The only thing for the daddies to do is to return to the ice. They gather slowly and as they catch their breath, and the acid leaves their bodies, they face a stark choice: Will they give up on their eggs, dive in again, or simply wait for the mommies to return?

It is our human actions that decide if the baby penguins will have time to hatch before the ice melts. If it will have time to learn to swim before the ice breaks. And we decide what the mommy penguin will see when she returns from the ocean. Emperor penguins did not create global warming, and they will not have time to adapt to it.

The story of the penguin is all about emotion and instinct. Unlike Thunberg's confrontational speech, this speech fosters identification: the process of building a connection with the audience by highlighting shared characteristics. In this case, the idea of the penguins as a family helps the audience identify with them. The speech does include numbers, but they are not what drives the story. You do not have to be a climate activist to understand it. You do not have to understand the climate science to feel the need to act to save the emperor penguins from extinction.

## MALALA YOUSAFZAI'S EMOTIONS

Emotionally compelling speeches do not require grand occasions. The context in which they are delivered can be quite ordinary—like commemorating the planting of a tree in a local community. I wrote exactly such a speech once. We were celebrating the two-hundred-year anniversary of the Danish law enabling all children to have an education and (a little delayed) the one-hundred-year anniversary of a women's right to vote.

The speech was centered on the story of Malala Yousafzai, an activist for gender equality in education who survived an assassination attempt. By using Yousafzai I could exemplify the importance of girl's education and equality in voting to an audience of primarily young children from the local school. The identification was even stronger as the speaker I wrote the speech for was a woman government minister who had grown up in that community. The children in the audience could see that the speaker had really achieved what Yousafzai was fighting for, and she represented what we were there to celebrate. The speech started this way:

> In Afghanistan lives a girl called Malala Yousefzai. Like you, she was also happy to go to school. She did not ride a bike, but the bus.
>
> When Malala was seventeen years old, the Taliban stopped her school bus. They entered with their machine guns, and they shot her in the head. For several months, she was in the hospital, but she survived. The Taliban

Since winning the Nobel Peace Prize, Malala Yousafzai has been invited to speak at many events, including the 2023 Nelson Mandela Annual Lecture in Johannesburg, South Africa.

shot her because she insisted that girls have a right to go to school.

Last year Malala won the Nobel Peace Prize and shared it with everybody who goes to school. Malala said that the prize belonged to "all who go to school." That is you!

In many places in the world people still struggle to go to school—to learn, to enhance, to grow. In Denmark we can go to school, and we have to appreciate that.

As you can see, you do not always need a big bag of rhetorical tricks. Sometimes a simple emotional story with a clear message and identification with the audience is all you need.

## MERLIN USES HIS EMOTIONS

Thunberg has been under a lot of critique for her emotional speaking, but her speech is only the most recent instance of a long and proud tradition. So long that it is the predominant norm throughout history. It is the emotionless argument that is the exception. Let us take a step back in time for a little perspective.

Most people know the legend of King Arthur and his Knights of the Round Table. Regardless of its historical accuracy, it is a testament to what persuasion might have looked like in the Middle Ages, when it was written. Allow me to introduce the setup. The fifteen-year-old Arthur draws the sword Excalibur from a rock by mistake, not knowing that he thereby becomes king. He discovers that he is the son of a former king, Uther Pendragon. This makes many noble men angry as they had their sights set on the throne or because they will not submit to the rule of a kid because of an old myth. As a result, Arthur quickly finds himself in the middle of a civil war.

And that is not all. Several rivals see an opportunity to get revenge on the father Arthur never knew. One of them is King Claudas, and he has good reason for revenge. Arthur's father destroyed his kingdom so thoroughly that it was known as the Land Laid Waste.

King Arthur is now in his twenties, and he has just married his sweetheart, Guinevere. The war with King Claudas is raging, and Claudas has twice as many men as Arthur. All the knights from the Round Table have fled with Arthur and hidden in the bushes off the battlefield. Merlin the Magician finds them there and gives a speech to bring them back to the battle. Here is the beginning of Merlin's speech:

What is happening? Have you come just to watch from here how good the men are at fighting?

You should know one thing. You have done something wrong: Many of our men have died because you rode away, and they are scared because they can't see you!

Now get going and ride against your enemies, and you will turn against them energized from your break here, so that anyone who might slip through your hands will say that they found worthy men and good knights here in Logres—not hired hands and stableboys.

And you—*Merlin turns to Arthur*—is this what your allies deserve? They have often risked their lives to help you out when you needed it the most and others failed you. Now you hide like a coward!

This is something that many people will often blame you for! And when your lady friend discovers what you did, she will scorn you for it!

Merlin's appeal is purely emotional: shame, pride, fear, honor, guilt. There are no numbers, cost-benefit analyses, or probabilities of victory. Merlin speaks directly to each knight to make sure the emotional appeal strikes their hearts. "You have done something wrong," "Your wife will scorn you for it," and "You hide like a coward," he says.

Merlin does not describe alternatives to hiding. He does not give a list of pros and cons. He tells them what to feel about hiding or fighting. And he does so by using his own emotions. The format fits the content.

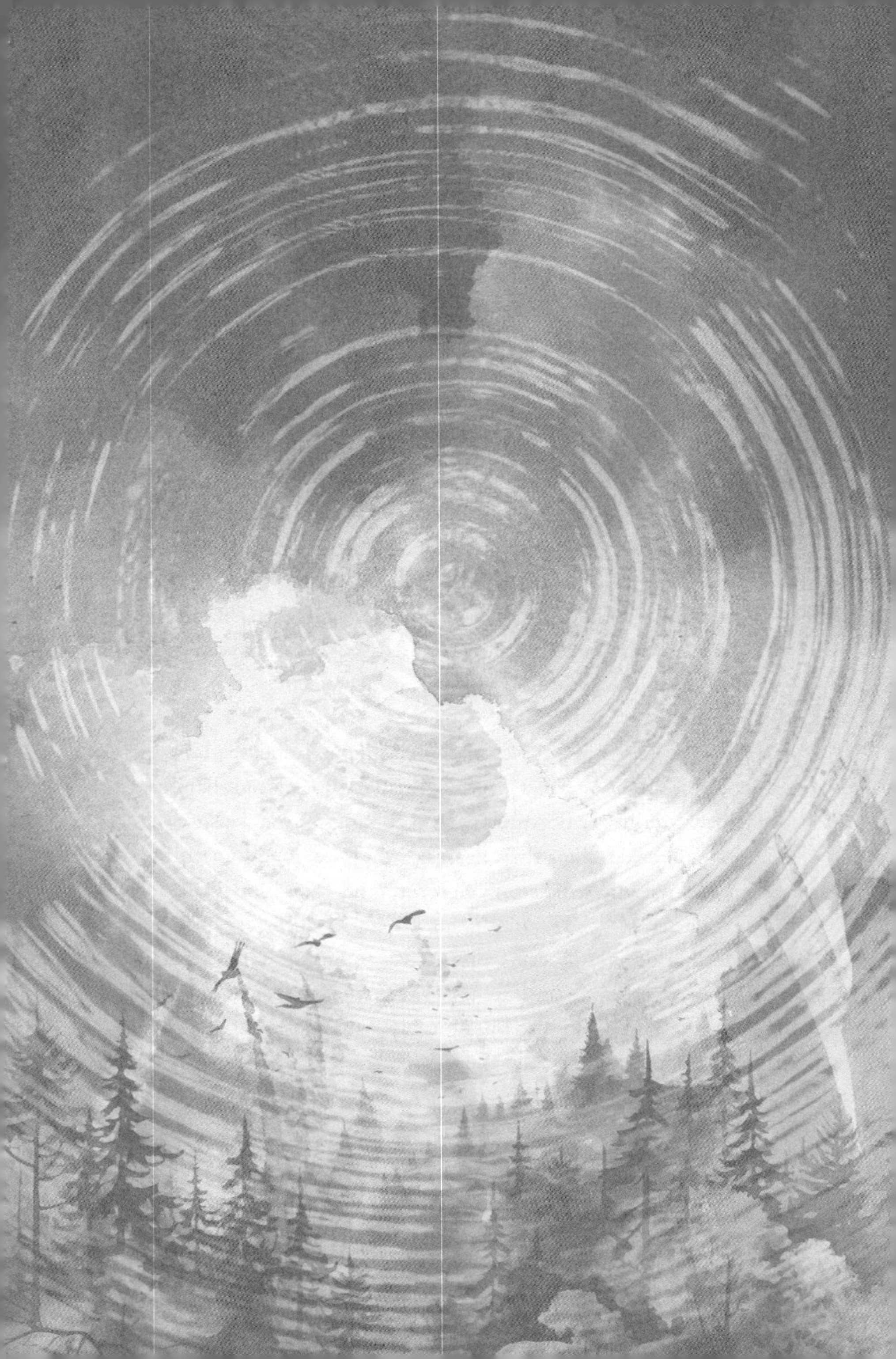

# CHAPTER 2
# BE TRUE TO YOUR WORLDVIEW

Your words express how you see the world, and the words of others show how they see it. You cannot get others to create the change you want if they do not understand your perspective. In a speech, you can convince them of your goals or at least provide nuance. Even if you think your perspective doesn't matter, your words could be the ones that resonate with someone and change their mind. And to be quite frank: If you are not true to your worldview, who will be?

Leading up to the decision on the Paris Agreement in 2015, Pope Francis gave a speech about climate. Using a canonical Catholic interpretation of the Bible, he argued that the environment has a right to exist and be healthy, that humans are a part of our environment, that to harm our environment is to harm people, that nature is God's creation with a value of its own, and no humans have a right to exploit that. He said, "We Christians, together with the other monotheistic religions, believe that the universe is the fruit of a loving decision by the Creator, who permits man respectfully to use creation for the good of his fellow men and for the glory of the Creator; he is not authorized to abuse it, much less to destroy it."

The pope's words highlight that we have to be true to our worldview—and adequately describe our relationship with nature.

In 2020 David Attenborough's documentary *A Life on*

*Our Planet* was released. It focused on the loss of biodiversity throughout the world. In the trailer for the film, Attenborough urges us to learn how to live with nature instead of against it. And in the book with the same title, he writes, "The natural world is fading. The evidence is all around. It's happened in my lifetime. I've seen it with my own eyes."

The year before, he elaborated the point to BBC Science: "You, me, and the rest of the human species are critically dependent on the health of the natural world. If the seas stop producing oxygen, we would be unable to breathe, and there is no food that we can digest that doesn't originate from the natural world. If we damage the natural world, we damage ourselves."

On Earth Day, April 22, 2021, then US president Biden invited world leaders to a virtual Climate Summit. President Xi Jinping of China attended and made headlines with his speech and pledges. He said, "Since [the] time of the industrial civilization,

Pope Francis (*center*) stands next to Barack Obama (*right*) during his welcoming ceremony at the White House in September 2015.

mankind has created massive material wealth. Yet, it has come at a cost of intensified exploitation of natural resources, which disrupted the balance in the Earth's ecosystem, and laid bare the growing tensions in the human-nature relationship. In recent years, climate change, biodiversity loss, worsening desertification and frequent extreme weather events have all posed severe challenges to human survival and development."

Although they come from different backgrounds and perspectives, the head of the Catholic Church, renowned storyteller David Attenborough, and President Xi have each pointed out that we need to change human's relationship with nature. And they are not alone.

You have to be true to the way you see the world and fight for what you believe. If you think the world is facing an existential threat—a catastrophe—in the form of global warming, then your choice of words, style, and pictures should reflect that view. Unless you are a scientist, graphs and averages represent the perspective of someone else. Terms such as "climate change" came from other people as well. You do not have to invent your own words, but be mindful that these words have been used by others who may have different views than you have.

Choosing words and ideas that reflect your position is called framing. Frames can be used to persuade people to any given position. As a speaker, you must make sure that position is in line with your ideas. In his book *Don't Think of an Elephant*, George Lakoff describes frames as mental structures that shape our ways of understanding the world. Framing is the art of communicating to activate specific ideas and associations. By being conscious about framing, we can activate relevant values and enable the audience to think within the framework of our worldview. So the framing you use has a direct effect on how the audience thinks about the topic.

Many climate speeches fail to frame the issue properly,

George Lakoff, a professor of linguistics at the University of California, Berkeley, speaks to the San Ramon Valley Democratic Club on February 25, 2010.

giving rise to what has been called scale mismatch. To convey the gravity of the climate crisis, people talk about mass extinctions and doomsday scenarios, but often the only solution they have is something like "change your light bulbs." The audience is left disillusioned and without adequate avenues for action. They experience a gulf between the consequences they face and the choices they have. They are left wondering: Is it the scenario or the solution that does not fit? How can a light bulb be the solution to an incoming catastrophe? And so they do nothing. The gulf between challenge and action is simply too great.

When we are talking about a complete, transformational restructuring to a zero-carbon world economy, we must choose our words wisely. If you talk about a crisis, you need to talk about the things we can do to cope. If you speak of an emergency, it requires urgent action. Yet the most common frame speakers use is still the emotionless and overcautious "climate change."

## FRAMING FOR INACTION

In November 2000, Bush was elected president of the United States. He was in close competition with then vice president Gore. The presidential election had, as they usually do, posed Bush and Gore as opposites. Gore was accused of being an environmentally conscious, elitist know-it-all, and Bush was the former alcoholic, oil-happy cowboy from Texas. After entering the White House in 2001, it did not take long for Bush to withdraw the United States from the Kyoto Protocol that it had adopted four years before.

The Kyoto Protocol is an international treaty on climate change named after the Japanese city of Kyoto, where it was negotiated. It seeks to limit and reduce greenhouse gas emissions in line with set targets, but the targets each country must reach are set by the countries themselves. The protocol is nonbinding and simply urges countries to create policies and report on progress.

At the time "global warming" was the term used in most speeches—including those by Bush. The term evoked an image of a burning world, giving a sense of a rising urgency. The public was pressuring Bush to do something about it, but he didn't want to stop using fossil fuels. He needed a way to talk about climate without getting people to demand political action. How could he make people *not* care?

To answer that question, Bush hired Frank Luntz. Luntz was a consultant for the Republican Party tasked with helping the politicians find the words for their ideas to get the popular backing they needed. Since 1995 he had researched what people heard when politicians spoke, including on climate, the environment, and energy, and in 1998 he was invited to talk about environmental framing at a Republican Senate conference. He knew that they would want proof for the advice on effective communication he was about to give, and so he came up with a way to give them that.

He wrote a speech about environmental issues, had four

Frank Luntz is a communication consultant for businesses and politicians. He is well known for his collaboration with the Bush campaign and other Republican politicians.

senators deliver it, and recorded them on video. He showed the four videos to a focus group of swing voters, people who were undecided about whether they would vote for Democratic or Republican candidates, and had them do an instant response dial session, where each participant had a remote control with a button that could be adjusted to a number between 1 and 100. The participants were to evaluate each statement second by second by dialing if they liked or disliked it and how much. The data would provide an instant graph of the intensity of people's reaction to what is said. And that graph could be displayed alongside the video recording of the speech.

Luntz collected the data and brought the recordings to the conference. He had divided the speech into sections and showed the different versions of each section alongside the respective graph of the audience's reactions. Then the conference attendees could compare the different versions of the same segment and see the polled population reaction in real time.

The message was clear. It did not matter if the senator was male or female, a good or a bad speaker, or if they had an accent. The audience reacted positively and strongly to good language—and good language was good framing, as you will see set out in the brief Luntz produced for Bush and the Republicans in 2002.

Luntz's 2002 brief set the standard for climate communications for years to come. In the brief, Luntz argued that Republicans so far had "lost the environmental communications battle." His solution was to put the weight of the argument on uncertainty and lack of scientific consensus: "'Climate change' is less frightening than 'global warming.' As one focus group participant noted, climate change 'sounds like you're going from Pittsburgh to Fort Lauderdale.' While global warming has catastrophic connotations attached to it, climate change suggests a more controllable and less emotional challenge."

Bush was encouraged to avoid using scary concepts such as global warming and replace them with "climate change." "Climate change" sounds neither scary nor urgent. "Change" is neutral. It sounds nice, even attractive. That is how the threatening global warming with extreme weather events was made to sound like early summer or a pleasant trip down south. The brief urged Republicans to argue for delaying action until all the facts were on the table.

Bush took it to heart. He rarely mentioned global warming after 2002, and he maintained that while climate change did exist, it was impossible to know if humans had caused it or if it was natural. In his State of the Union speech in 2008, he launched a plan for a fund to combat climate change through technology, but he also rejected all international agreements with the argument that they only work if everybody joins—entirely following Luntz's brief as it states: "The 'international fairness' issue is the emotional home run. Given the chance, Americans will demand that all nations be part of any international global warming treaty. Nations such as China, Mexico and India would have to sign such an agreement for the majority of Americans to support it."

And so the United States would wait until all other governments joined. And so did everybody else. As a result, nothing really happened.

Even after Bush left office, US action on climate was minimal. Obama's speechwriter Jon Favreau is famous for saying that the stories mean more than the words. Maybe that is why Obama adopted Bush's use of "climate change." But, by using the same words that Luntz said would sow doubt in the American public, Obama inadvertently perpetuated the problem. Republicans continued to insist that scientists hadn't found a consensus, and when Trump made it to the White House in 2016, even "climate change" was being framed as a hoax. The Luntz brief was still the manual to follow.

## THE TACTICS OF CLIMATE EMERGENCY SKEPTICS AND DENIERS

We have to consider how our messages and metaphors are received by our audience. And when talking about climate communication, we need to be aware of the pitfalls and tactics used by climate skeptics and science deniers. This is the playbook built on the Luntz brief:

**The first tactic is to remove focus from climate science by calling it a question of religion or faith.** If climate activism is framed as a religion, then it will sound preposterous and illogical—despite one hundred years of climate science backing it up. Framing the issue this way will also remove climate from the political realm, where governments can enact policies and mobilize large-scale solutions, and make it a private or individual issue, where each person has very little power to make a big difference.

**The second tactic is appealing to uncertainty.** The future is always uncertain, and by definition, we do not know what will happen: the situation might improve or decline. Climate deniers use this to postpone action, despite countless scientific reports and the existence of very real climate consequences in the present. This argument sows doubt in the possible future scenarios proposed by scientists on the IPCC, which are based on enormous amounts of data, and is used to keep unpleasant decisions at a distance.

**The third tactic is conspiracy theories and straw man fallacies.** Straw man fallacies are a rhetorical technique where someone distorts or misrepresents an opponent's argument or position to make it easier to attack or refute. Instead of focusing on the science or the political actions to take, the spotlight is put on the scientist or activist as a person. Climate activism and climate science are being portrayed as politically controlled or financially motivated: "It is all a hoax" or "They are just saying that to get more money." In this way, claims of scientific consensus is taken to mean the oppression of alternative views. And for the same reason, when journalists are inviting in "both sides" of a science debate that really does not have two sides, the result is an undermining of the scientific consensus by equaling it to an opinion. And leaving out what some would consider one side of the argument opens the door to accusations of conspiracy or personal motives.

**The fourth tactic is diversion.** The climate crisis is all-encompassing, and it will cost a lot of money. The longer we delay action, the more it will cost. And all that money could be used for something else (if you believe that inaction does not also have a price). So climate deniers will shift focus from climate to all the things they would rather use money on. The point is to pit climate action against fighting malaria, child mortality, or AIDS—or COVID-19, jobs, and the economy. What this tactic leaves out of the equation is how those very issues will develop in a world without climate action. In such a world, malaria would expand rapidly, child mortality will rise, many diseases will be harder to treat, pandemics could return, jobs will be lost, and the economy will suffer. But they will have us talk about anything but climate action.

## GRETA THUNBERG'S FRAMING IS TRUE TO HER WORLDVIEW

That was the situation when Greta Thunberg made it to the world stage by organizing the School Strike for Climate in 2018, an event where students all across the world walked out of school in protest of the lack of government action in response to the climate crisis. In January 2019 she spoke at the World Economic Forum in Davos, Switzerland. "Our house is on fire. I am here to say our house is on fire," she said. She ended the speech with the same metaphor: "I don't *want* your hope. I don't want you to be hopeful. I want you to panic. I want you to feel the fear I feel every day. And then I want you to act. I want you to act as you would in a crisis. I want you to act as if the house was on fire. Because it is."

"The house is on fire" is an urgent metaphor. There is no time to wait for all the facts to emerge or to fight over who will start or to discuss who will pay or to invent new solutions to better stop the flames. When a sixteen-year-old girl stands before world leaders and talks about the future she lost as a result of their inaction, it is an emotional and moral argument for climate action. It is the setup to an emotional story, making it impossible to defend inaction with common sense or sound science.

In at least three ways, Thunberg became the antidote to the Luntz brief, turning rhetoric such as Trump's against itself:

1. **An emotionally compelling story beats cold hard facts.**

The Luntz brief told politicians to "think of environmental (and other) issues in terms of 'story.' A compelling story, even if factually inaccurate, can be more emotionally compelling than a dry recitation of the truth."

Thunberg is not afraid to show her own feelings and appeal to the emotions of her audience. That is impactful communication because she does not simply *tell* a story—she *is* the story. The story of a Swedish teenage girl who went on a school strike and started a global youth movement for climate action. She takes the old communication axiom "Show, don't tell," one step further. She said, "Adults keep saying, 'We owe it to the young people to give them hope.' But I don't want your hope. I don't want you to be hopeful. I want you to panic."

**2. Convince your audience that you are on their side.**

Luntz asserted that "the first (and most important) step to neutralizing the problem and eventually bringing people around to your point of view on environmental issues is to convince them of your sincerity and concern."

When Thunberg gives a speech, there is no doubt what she wants to happen, and you know she is sincerely concerned about the future. It is also clear that she speaks for a large group of young people demanding adequate climate action. She is credible, sincere, and concerned on behalf of all of us. For example, she said, "We are now at a time in history where everyone with any insight of the climate crisis that threatens our civilization and the entire biosphere must speak out in clear language, no matter how uncomfortable and unprofitable that may be. We must change almost everything in our current societies. The bigger your carbon footprint is, the bigger your moral duty. The bigger your platform, the bigger your responsibility."

3. **Sowing doubt about the facts will undermine the urgency and stall action.**

Luntz believed that "the most important principle in any discussion of global warming is your commitment to sound science."

In this third principle, Luntz sows doubt about the facts by contrasting them with "sound science" much like the use of "common sense" as opposed to scientific results. Thunberg goes straight to urgency and the need for action with the metaphor "the house is in fire." She avoids the trap of making it a discussion of different understandings of science. She ends that discussion and leaves it for the opponent to "follow the science," whether it is the facts or sound science. While Luntz and Bush appeal to "sound science" as opposed to the scientific consensus, Trump ignores the science completely, and Thunberg takes it as a given. The lesson is that science doesn't push people to take a stand, either for or against climate change. How the speaker makes you feel about the science does.

In 2010 Luntz changed. Now he advocates for bipartisan climate action. He claims he was wrong, and in 2019, he asked people to stop using the brief he wrote eighteen years ago because it's not accurate today. Unfortunately, his points are still used to delay climate action.

## AN EXISTENTIAL THREAT AND HUMANS' WAR ON NATURE

Thunberg's frank, impassioned speech resonated with people all around the world and made an impact on how US politicians began talking about the issue. The 2020 presidential election in the United States was also a choice between worldviews. In September 2020, Biden became the official Democratic candidate for president

In 2023 Kamala Harris spoke at the COP28 Climate Conference in Dubai, United Arab Emirates. She described US climate policies under the Biden administration and its commitment to support climate action.

of the United States. In his speech after being nominated, he spoke about "the existential threat posed by climate change," and his Clean Energy Revolution plan noted that "there is no greater challenge facing our country and our world."

In June 2019, then VP candidate Kamala Harris was asked about "climate change" and she answered, "I don't even call it climate change. It's a climate crisis."

At a White House event on August 1, 2022, she expanded and said that "Climate change has become a climate crisis. And a threat has now become a reality." thereby enforcing the idea of "climate as security."

Allow me to go back a little. In the beginning of March 2014, Russia annexed the Crimean Peninsula in Ukraine. Even before that, tension had been building as the then president of Ukraine sought to ally with Russian president Vladimir Putin and move away from the European Union. The Euromaidan protests erupted as a consequence. Yet Ukraine and large swaths of eastern Europe were wholly dependent on Russian natural gas. At the time I was the speechwriter in the Danish Ministry for Climate, Energy and Buildings. And I saw firsthand how European climate politics collided and became a matter of national security—and thus moved from *nice-to-have* to *need-to-have*.

After the Russian invasion of Ukraine some eight years later the frame "climate as security" has demonstrated its potential. Sweeping political plans and massive investments have been pointed toward energy independence. Yet energy independence will not stop the global impacts of the climate crisis if we simply switch foreign fossil fuels with locally produced fossil fuels. "Climate as security" must encompass both security through local supply and security from global impact—as when Biden called the climate crisis "an existential threat."

In the summer of 2024, the Democrats and the Republicans held party conventions to nominate presidential and vice-presidential candidates. At the Republican National Convention in July, climate was almost nonexisting. It was mentioned mainly indirectly when attacking the Democrats for taking away ordinary people's freedom to choose their own source of energy. It was a freedom from regulation argument.

At the Democratic National Convention in August, mentions were few and far between. Yet Obama attacked Trump for thinking that "freedom means that the powerful can do pretty much what they please . . . put poison in our rivers." And he spoke about "a broader idea of freedom" including the "freedom to breathe clean air and drink clean water."

Presidential candidate Kamala Harris also mentioned "the freedom to breathe clean air, drink clean water, and live free from the pollution that fuels the climate crisis." It was a "freedom from the impacts of the climate crisis" argument.

The common term seems to be "climate as freedom." And vice-presidential candidate for the Democratic Party, Tim Walz, expanded on it. He said, "Freedom. When Republicans use the word freedom, they mean that . . . [corporations should be] free to pollute your air and water. . . . But when we Democrats talk about freedom, we mean the freedom to make a better life for yourself and the people that you love."

The public debate about climate has moved considerably from "change"—crisis to threat to security to freedom. Yet Lakoff has consistently argued that climate should be framed as freedom at least since his book was published in 2004. According to him, when we talk about climate, we should talk about protecting fundamental freedoms from the threat of climate impacts and making sure that we may thrive in a stable environment.

The way we talk about climate has changed dramatically. From Bush setting the stage by calling it "climate change" to avoid pressure to act, and Gore popularizing the term "climate crisis" to highlight the need to act with enforcements from the United Nations, and Thunberg pushing for recognizing it as a "climate emergency." To Biden calling it "an existential threat" as part of a wider "climate as security" in Europe too with the threat to energy and sovereignty. And—maybe, now—"climate as freedom" with a political fight to define that freedom as being "freedom from government climate regulation" or "freedom from the impacts of climate."

But does the term "climate crisis" capture what you think of the climate? Does it fit your worldview? Or is what you see better described as a "climate emergency" as used by Thunberg, the United Nations, and the European Union? It is important to be careful with your words because different concepts and metaphors activate different feelings, values, and worldviews. And different concepts point to different actions and solutions. Find the words that reflect how you see the world but also be mindful that different metaphors and concepts have different strengths and weaknesses.

On December 2, 2020, the UN report titled "The State of the Planet" was launched at Columbia University in New York City, and UN secretary general António Guterres gave a speech. This is the beginning of his speech: "To put it simply, the state of the planet is broken. Dear friends, humanity is waging war on nature. This is suicidal. Nature always strikes back—and it is already doing so with growing force and fury. Biodiversity is collapsing. One million species are at risk of extinction."

Guterres's worldview comes across strongly. Humankind is at war with nature. We are on a suicide mission as a species. Gone is all talk of "climate change" or "climate crisis." Guterres speaks of "a climate catastrophe" with "apocalyptic fires and floods, cyclones and hurricanes," threatening a "climate cataclysm" and "our descent towards chaos." The climate has entered a war of almost biblical rhetoric.

But then Guterres talks about a race when he says that we are "in a race against time to adapt to a rapidly changing climate," and later, "the race to resilience is as important as the race to net-zero." The race metaphor is quite different from the biblical rhetoric of cataclysm, chaos, and the apocalypse.

At the end, Guterres urges us to "stop the plunder and start the healing." This is yet another metaphor different from "the apocalypse," "the war," or "the race."

Guterres's speech highlights the need to identify your own worldview and choose words that stick to that worldview. War metaphors are good at mobilizing support for acute and short-term action. They divide us into friend and enemy—us and them. But

Guterres delivered his speech about climate using strong metaphors to get his point across.

the climate crisis is a long and deep transition that will likely never stop. And when we are our own worst enemy, then how do we win? If we are in a suicidal war against nature, do we betray our species by taking climate action?

Furthermore, what if the battle is a biblical one, as suggested by the word "apocalyptic"? How do we know what side God is on? And do we even need to fight if God is on our side? Should we just wait and let God decide, or are we fighting against God? It can be hard to decide what to do, and in the end, war metaphors tend only to mobilize those that already agree with you. The rest will wait out the battle, focusing on survival—and confusion will likely grow that number.

Racing is also a commonly used metaphor for climate. Compared to a battle, a race tends to be less risky. Using this metaphor can mobilize for long-term action but likely with less engagement. Once the issue is a race, it is no longer a matter of life or death. Whether you win or lose, you get to race another day. Even coming in second place is not bad when compared to losing a war. But can we treat the climate crisis as a race to be won or lost and then try again?

Too many metaphors create confusion. And confusion creates inaction. We get lost in the ramifications of those metaphors and what they are each calling on us to do. But the climate crisis needs action, and it should not be left to those dedicated enough to fight in a battle, those eager or competitive enough to race, or those devoted enough to wage holy war.

In July 2023, Guterres launched a new metaphor with the ominous words: "The era of global warming has ended; the era of global boiling has arrived."

It is clear that boiling is escalated rhetoric from warming (which sounds nice in comparison), but what family of metaphor it belongs to is harder to identify. And that means that your audience cannot use your metaphor as a shortcut to understand your meaning—and the metaphor loses its power.

## LAKOFF AND LUNTZ VALUE THEIR WORDS

I have mentioned both George Lakoff and Frank Luntz in the chapter above. They are on opposite sides of the political debate, but they share a weapon: *framing*.

The title of Lakoff's book, *Don't Think of an Elephant*, plays on the paradox that if you ask people not to think of an elephant, all they can do is think of an elephant. This illustrates his point that because our audience will think of whatever we talk about, we should talk about what we want, not what we do not want. This is particularly important because repeated exposure to our worldview will make it more relatable, and the words we use carry values and stories.

Lakoff uses taxes as an example. If you say, "tax relief," you imply taxes are a burden. If taxes are an unjust burden that we all wish to be lifted, then the hero of the story will be the one providing us with tax relief. And with taxes as a burden, it is only rational for us to avoid taxes altogether, if we can. That is where "tax havens" come in. Who would not want to seek relief from a burden by going to a haven? That must be the goal. If laws, regulations, and certain politicians are preventing us from relieving our burden, then they are the villains of the story, and we must work to combat them. In this way, the simple metaphor of "tax relief" contains the structure of a whole story. Other words would communicate a different story. You could frame taxes as a loan, a contract, or an act of solidarity, and each would paint a different picture in your audience's mind.

On the last pages of Lakoff's book, he summarizes his guidance in four points:

1. Show respect.
2. Respond by reframing.
3. Think and talk at the level of values.
4. Say what you believe.

Be true to your worldview—when you listen with respect, when you respond through reframing, when you talk about (shared) values, and when you argue your case to make your point.

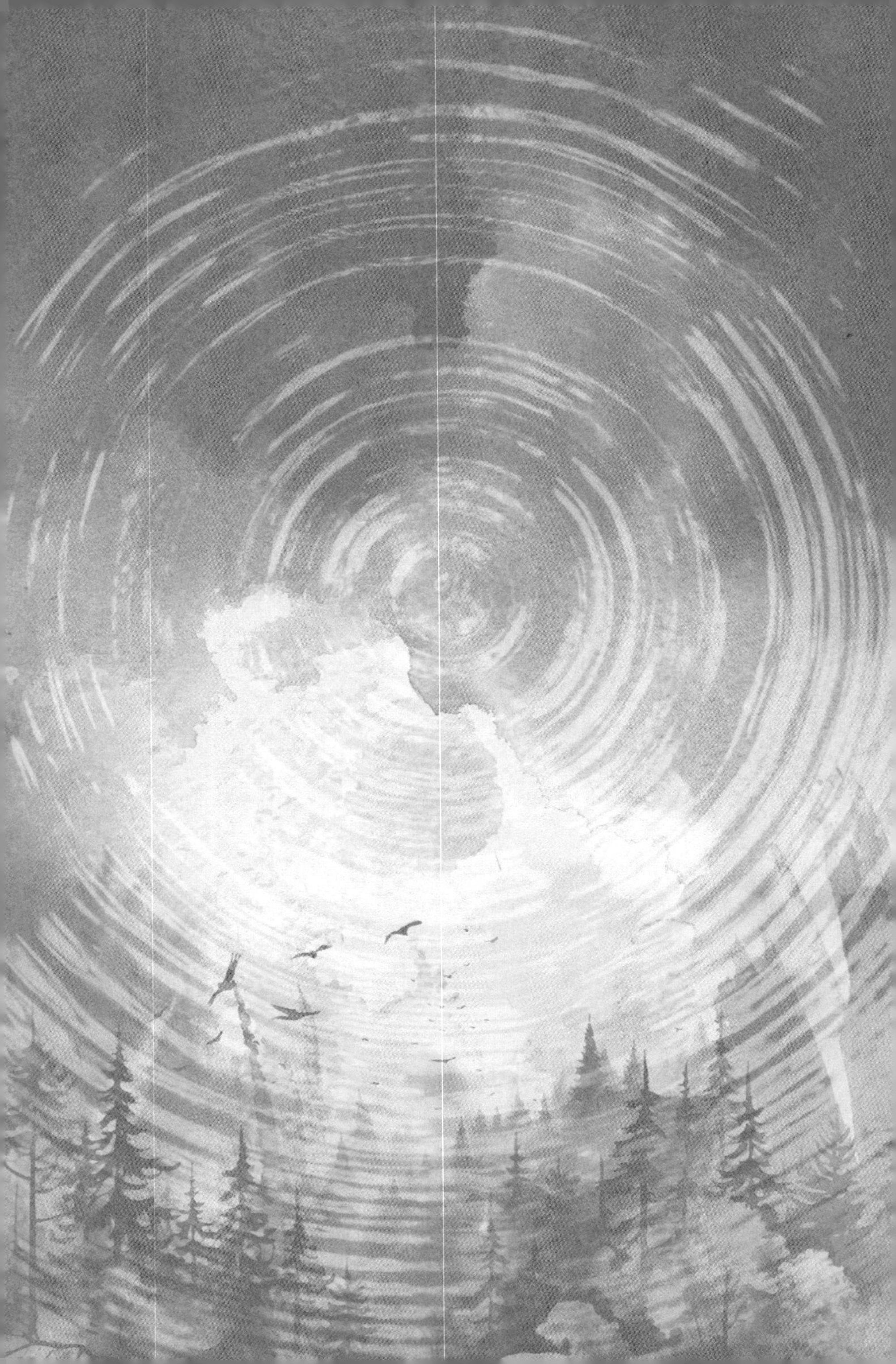

# CHAPTER 3
# FIND INSPIRATION IN THE PAST

We can't do it because we have never done it before. That is, unfortunately, how many people think, and it prevents them from taking action. You have to change that mentality with your speech. One of the biggest mistakes speakers make in mobilizing people for climate action is describing the climate crisis as exceptional, all-encompassing, and unique. This sets climate apart from our tools, knowledge, and experience, and thus the hope that we can do something about it. In a philosophical sense, any event will always be unique because it has never happened before exactly as it is happening now. And so when environmentalist Bill McKibben calls the climate crisis "the greatest crisis in the history of our species," he may be right.

When Thunberg states that "solving the climate crisis is the greatest and most complex challenge homo sapiens have ever faced," she may be right. But their words are ultimately counterproductive if they stand alone. By presenting the climate crisis as uniquely difficult to solve, they are taking away our chance to learn and find inspiration from past societal achievements.

The greatest barrier to action is the belief that we cannot change. This belief stems from ignorance of the past, and not knowing about our past limits our future. That is why urging people to change should always be accompanied by a story about how we've done this before. You have to show that many people

Clover Hogan was one of over four hundred speakers at the ChangeNOW 2023 conference.

have already taken action, that humans have revolutionized society many times throughout history, and that if we've done it once, we can do it again. Use the past for inspiration and hope.

"Shifting baseline" is a concept from biodiversity that describes how every generation of people judges the state of nature as compared to their previous experiences, or baseline. Each generation can clearly see how biodiversity has changed over their lifetime. The problem is that the baseline shifts gradually from generation to generation, and this shift is much harder to recognize. This leads people to believe that the changes aren't as dramatic and long-term as they really are—that the situation is not as urgent as it really is. Your role as a change-maker is to remind people that the world is not set in stone, to tell a story about how we have changed before, and to make the message stick that we can do it again.

At ChangeNOW—an international conference for leaders in climate solutions in Paris, France, in 2023—climate activist Clover Hogan gave an excellent example of this kind of message. She gave a speech about activism and pointed at the past to find inspiration. Hogan said, "The most insidious threat we face is not the assault of the fossil fuel industry but the illusion that people in power will stop them. History shows us that the opposite is true. In 1969 it was the queer community who resisted police brutality during the Stonewall uprising. In 1955 it was Rosa Parks who refused to give up her seat on the bus to a white man. In 1918 it was suffragettes who won the right for women to vote."

## THE HOLE IN THE OZONE LAYER

I remember learning about the hole in the ozone layer vividly from my own childhood. I turned six in 1985, and I hated sunscreen like the plague. The very thought that there was a hole in the ozone layer above us and that it meant I had to put sunscreen all over my body was horrific. Sunscreen quickly became a cuss word, and even today, I feel a gut reaction to the mere mention of it. But the story of the hole in the ozone layer did not start in the 1980s. It is much older than that.

The atmosphere has been pondered by scientists since at least the eighteenth century. In 1774 Joseph Priestley discovered oxygen, and in the name of experimental physics, someone set it on fire and found that it smelled. In 1849 Christian Friedrich Schönbein called this smelly oxygen "ozone" after the Greek word for smell, "ozein." Other scientists discovered that ozone was a gas made from three oxygen atoms. In 1913 Charles Fabry and Henri Buisson measured the ozone in the atmosphere with a device called an interferometer and found that ozone gathered in a layer in the stratosphere some 12 to 18 miles (20 to 29 km) aboveground, where it protects us from the ultraviolet rays of the sun. The layer of ozone protects us from dangerous rays. So far, so good.

In 1924 meteorologist Gordon Dobson invented the Dobson ozone spectrophotometer, allowing scientists to measure the thickness of the ozone layer. Years later, they discovered that the thickness was not constant, and they wondered if it was being damaged by supersonic airplanes and space rockets traveling through the stratosphere. If so, it would have dire consequences for life on Earth. Suddenly, there was a threat to the ozone layer.

April 22, 1970, was the first Earth Day in the United States. It gathered the majority of the environmental movement, and it shifted focus from local action to global issues. Establishing Earth Day took a whole lot of coordination and cooperation between many organizations—and it happened because of the threat to the ozone layer. A coalition led by the environmental groups Sierra Club and Friends of the Earth created a campaign focused on opposing supersonic airplanes to protect the ozone layer. The coalition asked people to write letters to their elected officials urging them to vote against supersonic airplanes on the grounds that they were too expensive, used too much energy, were noisy, and threatened the ozone layer.

Leaders of the coalition spoke to Congress in Washington, DC, gave depositions at political hearings, and met with several decision-makers directly. The government support for supersonic airplanes was halted. Their success taught the coalition that they could have an impact on global issues, leading more environmental groups to coordinate actions and collaborate internationally.

Meanwhile, independent scientist James Lovelock had been wondering about something from the front of his cottage on the western coast of Ireland. He had grown tired of the smog blocking his view and wanted to determine where it came from. He decided to measure the chemicals in the atmosphere in the industrial part of town. It turned out that massive amounts of chlorofluorocarbon (CFC) gases were coming from the chimneys.

CFCs are a type of industrial chemical developed in the late 1920s by the American company General Motors to replace toxic gases in common household products. Their chemical structure makes them effective coolants. They were used in deodorants, hair spray, refrigerators, air-conditioning units, Styrofoam cleaning detergents, and fire extinguishers. Since they served multiple functions, were cheap to produce, and were thought to be harmless compared to their predecessors, they spread from the United States to Europe, China, Latin America, and Asia.

Lovelock was concerned by what he saw. To compare his finding to somewhere without chimneys, he measured the sky above the Atlantic Ocean. That air was supposed to be clean. But Lovelock measured CFCs—even on days without smog and with a clear view. It made Lovelock curious, and when chance arose in 1972, he paid for a trip on a research vessel to Antarctica. He brought the device along and measured CFCs on the way. There were CFCs everywhere—even in the pristine sky above Antarctica, a continent without human inhabitants, cities, or industry.

Later that year, Lovelock attended a conference and spoke about his findings. Frank Sherwood Rowland, a chemist interested in CFCs, attended Lovelock's presentation. Inspired by Lovelock's work, Rowland wondered how CFCs might react under extreme conditions in the atmosphere. Would they stay CFCs, or would they react with other substances and transform into something else? Rowland teamed up with fellow chemist Mario Molina, and their analysis concluded that as long as they remained in the lower atmosphere, CFC gases wouldn't change into other substances. But CFCs were subject to storms, wind, and changes in density in the atmosphere. They would not remain in the lower atmosphere; they would rise even higher. And, Rowland and Molina figured, at some point the CFCs could rise to a height where the rays of the sun were so strong that they would turn the CFC gases into more basic elements such as chlorine.

That left them with this question: What would happen with

the chlorine in the atmosphere? In the laboratory, they tried mixing chlorine with ozone and found that a single molecule of chlorine could destroy as many as one hundred thousand ozone molecules. Rowland and Molina were concerned by these results. Tons of CFCs were in the atmosphere, and they would rise until the sun turned them into chlorine. The chlorine would then destroy the ozone layer that protected us from the dangerous rays of the sun. Even a little CFC gas was a significant threat to the ozone layer.

The manufacturing companies that used CFCs were unhappy about these findings. This industry, after all, had a turnover of $50 billion in 1974 and represented two hundred thousand jobs. They tried to make the case that Rowland and Molina's discovery was just a theory, even paying a critic to go on a speaking tour arguing against it.

The environmental movement pushed back. They started a campaign informing the public about the hole in the ozone layer and pushing for a massive boycott of products containing CFCs. Friends of the Earth launched a campaign to remove CFCs. It worked. In the United States, nonessential CFCs were made illegal in 1978, and Canada, Norway, and Sweden followed with their own bans soon after. Yet even though production fell, it wasn't enough, and production of CFCs began to rise again in the 1980s.

But the story was still evolving. In 1982 a research ship was approaching Antarctica. On board were researchers Susan Solomon and Joe Farman, who had brought along a Dobson ozone spectrophotometer to measure the thickness of the ozone layer above Antarctica. Farman had gathered atmospheric data from Antarctica for twenty-five years. But this year his data showed less ozone than expected—it was less than half. Farman didn't believe it. He thought there had to be a malfunction in his equipment, so he brought a new set of devices the year after. But the hole in the ozone was still there. Farman looked at data from the previous

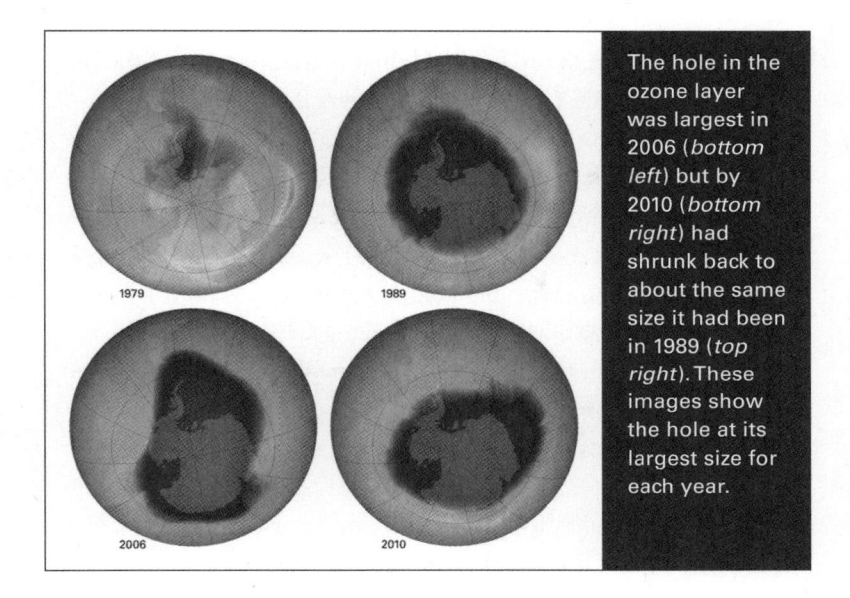

The hole in the ozone layer was largest in 2006 (*bottom left*) but by 2010 (*bottom right*) had shrunk back to about the same size it had been in 1989 (*top right*). These images show the hole at its largest size for each year.

years, and he found the hole had been there since 1977. Then he measured in other places in Antarctica, and the hole was still there. When he returned, he told officials at the National Aeronautics and Space Administration (NASA) about his results. NASA took a second and more detailed look at the data from Antarctica—and measurements that had previously been interpreted as malfunctions or gotten lost in averages were indications of a giant hole in the ozone layer about the size of the United States. The only possible cause for such a huge decrease in ozone over such a short period of time was CFCs.

Later that year, the United Nations gathered in Vienna, Austria, to discuss what to do. They agreed on the problem and the need for action, but not on the method and level of ambition. A huge part of southern Europe's economy relied on CFC production. The Soviet Union, then a group of republics that included Russia, needed CFCs for cooling in their southern provinces. The Japanese economy was centered on the production of microchips, and they used CFCs to clean them. In the United States, because of the law banning nonessential CFCs, manufacturers had begun finding alternatives, but a lot of jobs were still at stake.

Unable to reach a pragmatic solution, the United Nations agreed to meet again. Meanwhile, the hole would continue to grow. The environmental movement scaled up their campaign, asking people to boycott products and companies using CFCs. It was so successful that companies started removing CFCs from products and processes before the US government made CFCs illegal. Even McDonald's promised to remove CFCs from packaging in 1987—after receiving an avalanche of letters from school kids as a part of the campaign.

In 1987 the United Nations finally came to an agreement. The resulting Montreal Protocol halved the use of CFCs beginning in January 1989 and was ratified by all 197 UN countries. Three years later, the United Nations strengthened the protocol by enacting a complete ban on CFCs in industrialized nations. Between 2000 and 2015, the hole in the ozone had been reduced by an area the size of India, and scientists expect it to be fully healed by 2050. But that is not all.

By preventing the ozone hole from growing larger, the Montreal Protocol has prevented millions of cases of fatal skin cancer and tens of millions of cases of nonfatal skin cancer and eye cataracts. In the United States, 6.3 million skin cancer deaths will have been avoided by 2065 and an estimated $4.2 trillion in health-care costs will have been saved.

After political regulation—and the full ban—led corporations to hunt for alternatives to CFCs, they created hydrofluorocarbons (HFCs). HFCs were not a threat to the ozone layer, but they are a greenhouse gas one thousand times stronger than $CO_2$, making them a significant contributor to the climate crisis. After ten years of negotiations, the countries that ratified the Montreal Protocol met again in Kigali, Rwanda, in 2016 to ban HFCs under a new protocol. The Kigali Amendment was in force by 2019 and is expected to prevent the equivalent of 135 billion tons (122 billion t) of $CO_2$ from entering the atmosphere, or 0.4°C (0.72°F) of global warming—by 2100.

We might learn several lessons from this story. We can draw hope that massive and systemic solutions have been put to use on global challenges. We might find inspiration in the way it was done without attempting to duplicate it one to one. And we might see that there are many roles to play in making that change happen—scientist, activist, business owner, politician, and ordinary citizen.

## THE PAST CAN INSPIRE US TO MAKE CHANGES

A mobilizing speech should mark an occasion, invite people to take action, and encourage fighting for one's values. It should acknowledge the situation you are in, look toward the future, and connect to what is worth fighting for from the past.

More than document it, rhetoric shapes the past with the present need in mind. It shapes the past to fit the present and create the future. When a community remembers and interprets shared past events, it shapes the group's identity by influencing how members perceive and relate to their past and present.

Many speeches on climate attempt to mobilize their audience by describing how awful the crisis is right now and how much worse it will become if we do nothing to stop it. By focusing on the scale and severity of the climate crisis, this kind of doomsday rhetoric makes the climate crisis look unprecedented and scary, leaving us without options or hope. It does the opposite of what a mobilizing speech should do. It makes the past irrelevant and the future unpredictable, and it leaves us unable to affect it.

The connection between past, present, and future has always been central to mobilization in social movements such as the Civil

Rights Movement, the labor movement, and the American Indian Movement. And one person who has been central to understanding mobilization is Marshall Ganz.

Ganz is the Rita E. Hauser Senior Lecturer in Leadership, Organizing and Civil Society at the Kennedy School of Government at Harvard University, where he teaches leadership, narrative, strategy, and organization in social movements. He draws on experiences from his time as an organizer for the Student Nonviolent Coordinating Committee and the United Farm Workers. He led the grassroots organization for the 2008 Obama for President campaign and continues to train organizers through the global Leading Change Network.

Ganz believes our present choices rest on how we remember the past and how we imagine the future. He uses his own story as illustration: "I also was raised on years of Passover Seders. There's a part in the Passover Seder when they point to the kids and say, 'You were a slave in Egypt.' I finally realized the point was to recognize that we were all slaves in Egypt and in our time that same struggle from slavery to freedom is always going on, that you have to choose where you stand in that."

There is a reason why pointing out the connection between past, present, and future works to mobilize people: it reminds us we can change the narrative, and by doing so, we change how we act in the world. Anthropologist Edward Bruner has studied this phenomenon in the changes in collective identities of Indigenous people of the Americas. He describes how a story shift occurred: what started with a simple retelling became reality.

In what Bruner calls the 1930s dominant story, Indigenous people's pasts are seen as glorious, the present as disorganized, and the future as assimilation. He talked to numerous elders eager to provide information about the glorious past. Later, in what he calls the 1970's dominant story, the past is viewed as oppression, the present as resistance, and the future as resurgence. To understand this shift, Bruner talked to young activists fighting for a better future. He said, "The past, present, and future are not only constructed but connected in a lineal sequence that is defined by systematic—if not casual—relations. How we depict any one segment of the sequence is related to our conception of the whole, which I choose to think of as a story."

What happened to create this shift? Bruner describes it as several factors in the times after World War II. The war brought many Indigenous people to the front lines as soldiers in the military. When they came back, they felt unrecognized for their contributions in the war and founded the National Congress of American Indians (NCAI) in 1944 to represent their interests and protect their tribal rights, land, and culture. In 1953 US government policies aimed to strip Indigenous people of their tribal citizenship and land, removing federal protection and treaty obligations. The Termination Era of the 1950s and 1960s saw the US government strip Indigenous rights and reverse policies previously expanding Indigenous self-determination and governance. In other places in the United States, the Civil Rights Movement was brewing.

Several tribal leaders convened at the American Indian Chicago Conference in 1961 to discuss the issues Indigenous Americans faced and to write a declaration of self-determination. After listening to the conservative faction of the conference, many young Indigenous people grew disillusioned with the leadership and formed the National Indian Youth Council. They rejected the belief that Indigenous people were disorganized and in need of paternalistic help from the government or that the future was inevitable assimilation into the majority.

In 1966 young Indigenous Americans Clyde Warrior and Melvin Thom had heard Stokely Carmichael's iconic Black Power speech. Two weeks later, they gate-crashed the National Congress of American Indians annual conference parade. They arrived in a car with slogans on the side: "Red Power, National Indian Youth Council," and "Custer Died for Your Sins" (a reference to Colonel George A. Custer, a US Army colonel who died along with all his soldiers in a battle against the Lakota in 1876 and the title of a subsequent book by Vine Deloria Jr. in 1969). That was the first time those words were uttered in the general public.

In effect, they changed their story, and in performing a new story, they changed how they acted in the world. They moved the glorious moment from the past to the future, and changed assimilation and disorganization to oppression and resistance. In the new story, their role changed from "waiting to disappear" to "fighting for a better future."

You can make the same change. It depends on what you highlight. But what past should you highlight? You should be able to find one that fits your purpose and your audience.

## COLUMBUS AND QUILOMBOS

Some stories are so celebrated that they become legends. Such is the story of Christopher Columbus discovering the American continent. But there are always more sides to the story, and every side has the potential for inspiring the present and future. According to conventional history, in 1492 Columbus found the New World, America. Only, he merely visited a few islands in the Caribbean (the Bahamas, Cuba, and Hispaniola), which already had people living there. Even ignoring the Indigenous inhabitants, the continent had previously been discovered by Viking explorers from Iceland and Greenland, who set up camp for a full year or two in Newfoundland, Canada, in 1021 CE.

What Columbus *did* do was start the European colonization of the Americas—and with it, the practice of large-scale human enslavement and international transportation. Thirty-four years after Columbus's voyage, Portugal transported the first enslaved Africans across the Atlantic Ocean to the new colonies. They solidified the transatlantic slave trade, and over 250 years, it brought twelve million Africans to the Americas as enslaved workers.

The story of Columbus has many perspectives. There is the perspective of the Europeans colonizing the Americas, fighting the Indigenous Americans, and transporting enslaved Africans across the sea—and eventually making slavery illegal. That is the dominant one. More recently, the perspective of the enslaved Africans, and what it was like to live your life in a system of slavery, has become more widespread. But there is another one. One that combined resistance from the enslaved Africans with the Indigenous Americans.

In 2006 I left for ethnographic fieldwork in the Brazilian city Salvador da Bahia to study the "movimento negro," or Brazil's equivalent of the Civil Rights Movement. Here I saw the importance of having an inspiring story about resistance and change from the past. The movement participants called it "the mythical quilombo philosophy," and it told a story completely different from the dominant one. It was a story starting not with the European discovery of land or even enslavement of Africans but with proud African kings and queens, mutiny on board the slave ships and rebellions by enslaved Africans—and the creation of their own republic, a quilombo, and defending it within the Amazon rainforest. This story is seen as a fight for justice, and it continues to inspire people.

This movement does not see themselves as descendants of slaves but as resistance fighters, freedom fighters, and quilombolas. A quilombola is someone living in a quilombo or a mocambo, a marooned community of people who escaped their life as enslaved

The movimento negro is still ongoing and in 2023 included demonstrations against police violence.

people on a plantation to live free in a community of like-minded others, away from the slave economy.

When the Portuguese started transporting enslaved Africans to Brazil in 1526, it did not take long for the first Africans to set up camp in what would become known as the self-governing Republic of Palmares. It consisted of Africans who had escaped slavery, and as it grew it attracted even more people. The story goes that the capital was on top of the mountain of Serra da Barriga in the present-day Brazilian state of Alagoas, surrounded by a giant bamboo forest. When it was at its largest, 15 percent of all people in Brazil lived in Palmares, and it became a power that could not be ignored. In 1605 the European colonizers started an almost hundred-year-long military campaign with annual attacks on the city to attempt to bring them back into slavery.

In this state of perpetual warfare, a boy was born. He was still a baby when he was abducted from Palmares during one of the annual raids in 1655. Upon returning to their settlement, the colonial soldiers gave the boy to a Catholic priest, who named him Francisco. The priest made sure that Francisco was taught languages, mathematics, and the Bible. Yet when the boy was fifteen, he ran away and joined Palmares again. The people in Palmares were shocked—they thought he had been killed. Francisco was renamed Zumbi and became a soldier in Palmares. With his knowledge about the Portuguese, he quickly became general of the combined Palmares forces under King Ganga Zumba.

In 1678 Ganga Zumba, old and tired of constant war, signed a peace deal with the Portuguese colonizers, ensuring that Palmares would surrender in exchange for freedom for all its inhabitants. But the deal was declined by the local leaders of Palmares. They wanted freedom for ALL the enslaved people in Brazil. Zumbi was part of the rebellion against Ganga Zumba's deal that led to the king's death, and Zumbi became the new king of Palmares.

The noncompromising line angered the local plantation owners, and in 1694 they gathered a much bigger force, combining Portuguese mercenaries and local soldiers. Together they marched toward Palmares. With cannons they broke through the bamboo barricades and conquered the city. Only a small group of quilombola warriors, led by Zumbi, escaped through the burning chaos to the jungle. Here they continued their resistance using guerrilla tactics for more than a year. But on November 20, 1695, Zumbi was caught, captured, and decapitated.

When I came to Brazil in 2006, protest marches were filling the street with demands for reparations for past exploitation and establishing racial quotas at universities. Zumbi's name was written on banners declaring "A IMORTALIDADE DE ZUMBI" (the immortality of Zumbi). Several hundred years after his death, the inspiration of Zumbi's story was very much alive and was evoked with the word quilombola.

## THE CLIMATE CRISIS AND "THE GREAT BATTLE OF OUR TIME"

In 2020 Democrat Biden beat Republican Trump in the election for president of the United States. In his victory speech, Biden said, "Americans have called on us to marshal the forces of decency and the forces of fairness. To marshal the forces of science and the forces of hope in the great battles of our time."

When using the phrase "battles of our time," Biden positions the climate crisis in a long line of other historic battles. It is no less enormous in scale, and it is still a threat to our very existence, yet it is no longer unique. It is one in several, and we have overcome the others, implying we can also overcome this one, the climate crisis.

Later in his speech, Biden revealed that the battles he had in mind were these:

- Abraham Lincoln's saving the Union by winning the Civil War (1961–1965)

- Franklin D. Roosevelt's crafting of the New Deal to get the United States out of the Great Depression (1929–1939)

- John F. Kennedy's setting the course toward the moon

- Barack Obama's campaign slogan saying, "Yes We Can!"

The Obama reference might seem out of place, but using the catchphrase "Yes We Can" and Obama as a symbol, Biden is saying, *Yes we can* enact the change we need, because we have done

US president-elect Joe Biden delivers his victory speech after defeating Donald Trump in the 2020 US presidential election.

it before. We can use the inspiration from the past to shape the present and create the future.

It is no random phrase either. Since his presidential campaign, Biden has gotten help with speechwriting from historian Jon Meacham. Meacham wrote the speeches for Biden when he was nominated at the Democratic National Convention in August 2020, when he won the election in November, and when he declared climate change an existential threat in December. As a historian, Meacham knows the importance of the past as a mobilizing force for change in the present. Shortly before the US presidential election, he published the book *His Truth Is Marching On* about the civil rights icon John Lewis and how Lewis was inspired by another historical figure, Martin Luther King Jr. Much as Lewis drew from King's legacy, Meacham helped Biden draw from his predecessors.

Even using the battle metaphor was inspired by a familiar source: Gore. On September 20, 2019, Gore penned an op-ed in the *New York Times* with the headline: "The Climate Crisis Is the Battle of Our Time, and We Can Win." "Battle of our time" is a war metaphor combined with the idea of one defining battle for each generation. As we saw in the previous chapter, however, battle and war metaphors are tricky. How do you define the borders between generations, and how do you limit a generation to one defining battle? In Gore's op-ed, these "battles" go all the way back to ancient Greece, and there are no less than five "life or death challenges" just during World War II.

In Biden's speech there is a whole list of "inflection points" for that very moment, ranging from the climate crisis to COVID-19, the economy, health insurance, racism, common decency, democracy, and justice.

The war metaphor can be effective in mobilizing people for short-term all-or-nothing battles, as long as they agree with the goal and feel included in the groups being mobilized. But with five, or even eight, battles to choose from, what are they really mobilizing for? Your audience may get confused about where to direct their response. "Battles of our time" also has a biblical connotation related to the stories of the Apocalypse and Armageddon, because what will happen if we do not win the battles of our time?

Here the *quilombo* philosophy and lineage are stronger. They see themselves as standing on a history of strength, yet all is not over if they do not win right now. There will be another day and another battle. They cannot opt out of the battle, as they are a *quilombola* by definition as descendants of Africans in Brazil. It does not rest on a choice.

Throughout the climate movement, rhetoric has a tone of nostalgia. It sounds almost primal—like an echo of something long ago. An atmosphere fundamentally altered by burning fossil fuels. A planet desperately crying for survival. A fight for our future. An existential threat and a battle of our age. A growing tension in the human-nature relationship challenging human survival. Humanity's suicidal war on nature. A fading natural world. Stolen dreams. Our house is on fire. The era of global boiling has arrived.

These are words pointing to a bleak future. But they are also words pointing backward to the past—an echo.

In Thunberg's anger is an echo of Severn Cullis-Suzuki's twenty-five years before. Thunberg's "The house is on fire" is an echo of Gro Harlem Brundtland's "the Library of Life is burning" and of something more distant—maybe "the Tree of Life burning" from Norse mythology. In the tense relationship between humans and nature deteriorating into a suicidal war and ending in a boiling world is something else, something hidden. The metaphors are built on known images and tropes from the past. And there is a lesson here: we have faced devastating challenges before—and we might learn from them.

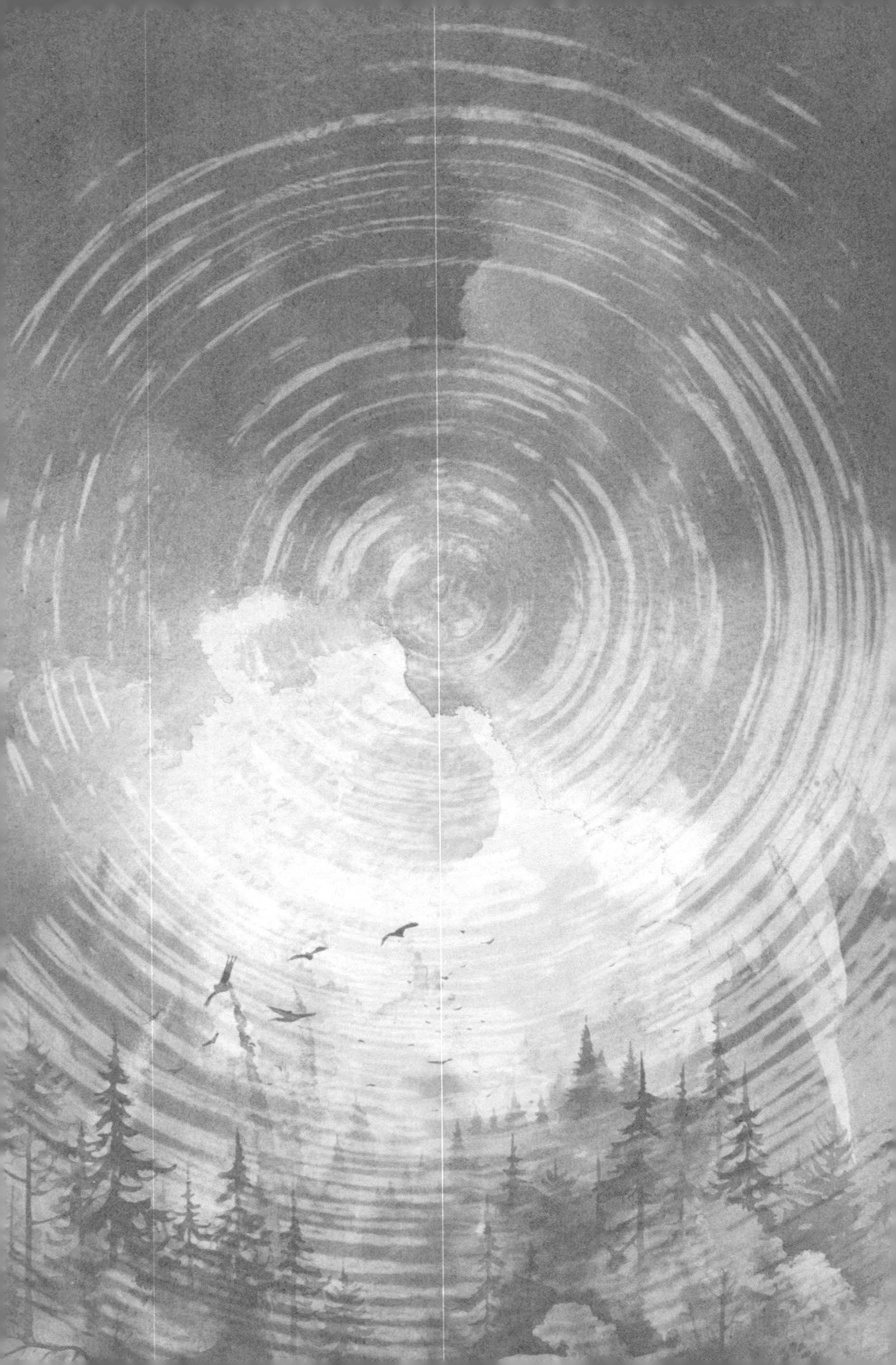

# CHAPTER 4
# BUILD A GOLDEN BRIDGE

"Build a golden bridge for your opponents to retreat across."
This is a quote often attributed to the Chinese philosopher of war Sun Tzu, but he did not say that. It is even hard to say where in his book *The Art of War* this quote was presumably taken from.

Yet it is good advice when you want your enemy to retreat and flee, but if you want to persuade them to join your cause, you cannot surround them on three sides—you can only make the one side more attractive. If you want people to move, you must make it appealing, safe, and easy to do so. That is the golden bridge you must build.

And as with all bridges, building a golden one starts with finding the spot with the shortest distance between two sides. By seeing where your values overlap, your audience will better identify with you and relate to your message. Everybody has a reason to care about the climate. The climate crisis tends to divide people into two camps along political lines—one believing in urgently addressing human-made climate change and one believing it is a conspiracy. As the gulf between the two camps grows, so do the consequences of disagreeing with your camp. You risk losing your group, your friends, and the perception of consistency in your opinions. This division is the result of polarization, and it makes it much harder to persuade people when changing involves such a risk.

That is the reason you must make it easy and appealing to be convinced. More so, it should not feel like an act of convincing—but like taking the attitudes and opinions that your audience already have to their logical conclusions. That is what the golden bridge should aim to do.

## SPEECHWRITING AS BRIDGE-BUILDING

In 2007 I helped my good friend Özlem Cekic get elected to the Danish Parliament. Cekic was born in the Kurdish region in Türkiye and came to Denmark as an immigrant with her family—she was the first woman in parliament with an immigrant background. And it did not take long before her inbox was full of hate mail cursing her, threatening her, and urging her to "go home" to Türkiye. It took a heavy toll on her health. At first, she just deleted the emails. Then she started saving them and reporting the threats to the police. Sometimes the letters would come to her house, signaling that they knew where she lived. She got a secret address and took precautions to protect her family. She was even harassed by a neo-Nazi calling her phone constantly. Her son asked her, Why does he hate you?

Along with the advice of a friend, this question spurred a realization that she could reach out to those sending hate mail, threats, and harassment. She opened her email and chose one. Then she picked up the phone and called the number. He answered, and they met for coffee at his house. His coffee set was identical to hers, and they ended up talking for two and a half hours. It turned out they had a lot in common.

That was how she started having Dialogue Coffee with her haters. She did this while still serving in parliament, but since leaving office she has run the Bridge Builders Association's Centre for Dialogue Coffee full-time. She says that most people agree to meet up, and that she always meets at their home to establish trust. She also always brings food to have something to share right away.

Özlem Cekic bridges the gap between different groups with opposing opinions using conversational techniques and coffee.

One of the most important lessons she learned is that people on the other side of the political aisle are not much different from her—and they are just as scared of the other side as she was of them. The people she had coffee with expressed an overarching message of feeling powerless. They believed all the failures, hardships, and unfortunate incidents they encountered throughout life were the fault of the other side. This belief is what drives the demonization and polarization that we must instead bridge with personal empowerment.

Cekic has a few relevant lessons to share:

1. You might feel scared or as if you need to gather a lot of courage in reaching out, but so do the people who disagree with you. Acknowledge that change is hard for them too.

2. Don't judge others during conversations. Focus on what values, experiences, and feelings you have in common.
3. Stay classy and finish conversations in a positive way, because you are going to meet them again. A bridge can't be built in one day.

Cekic's approach might be for conversations, but we can use her lessons for speeches as well. We build bridges by acknowledging the humanity of our audience regardless of whether they believe and act different than we do. We acknowledge their feelings and realize change is hard. We prepare to come back to continue building our connection. We focus on commonality in the human experience, such as enjoying a cup of coffee. Then we use our shared understanding to speak about climate.

## MALALA YOUSAFZAI BUILDS BRIDGES

In chapter 1, I told the story of Malala Yousafzai through a speech by Kirsten Brosbøl, but Yousafzai herself is great at building golden bridges. She makes it easy to be convinced to join her cause. By building an attractive golden bridge, she effectively eliminates distance between herself and her audience, and she makes it so compelling to take the bridge that following her seems as if it is the only logical thing to do.

In 2013 the United Nations officially designated July 12, her birthday, as Malala Day. She gave a speech on the occasion. In this speech, she starts by thanking God and then moves on to no less than nine of the most recognized and honored figures in recent world history, saying, "This is the compassion that I have learnt from Muhammad—the prophet of mercy—Jesus Christ, and Lord Buddha. This is the legacy of change that I have inherited from Martin Luther King, Nelson Mandela, and Muhammad Ali Jinnah. This is the philosophy of non-violence that I have learnt

Malala Yousafzai delivers her speech before the United Nations Youth Assembly at the UN headquarters in New York.

from Gandhi Jee, Bacha Khan, and Mother Teresa."

By naming such inspirational figures from around the world, she establishes a past that we can relate to and values that we can identify with. But the message is also that we are in this together, regardless of where we draw our inspiration: these values transcend our differences.

When you are relating giants of history to your struggle, it can appear as though you are the culmination of that history. That might seem arrogant and self-centered, making it counterproductive in its attempt to relate to the audience. Yousafzai must build a bridge to include us all as the audience. She does that throughout the speech by making a point of widening the struggle: "Thousands of people have been killed by the terrorists and millions have been injured. I am just one of them. So here I stand . . . one girl among many. I speak—not for myself, but for all girls and boys. I raise up my voice—not so that I can shout, but so that those without a voice can be heard."

Here we have a past to find inspiration in. We have shared values. And we have a broad community of people represented by the speaker. This is a great setup for moving the audience from inactivity to activism. Yousafzai accomplishes that by bringing the speech back to the context of her speaking—and of the power of speaking up for what you believe in. She said, "No one can stop us. We will speak for our rights, and we will bring change through our voice. We must believe in the power and the strength of our words. Our words can change the world."

She ends the speech with the slogan that she made famous: "One child, one teacher, one pen, and one book can change the world."

Yousafzai's rhetoric positions each of us on the podium with her because she speaks for us. We are all activists just as long as we receive an education—with a teacher, a pen, and a book. By implication, a lot of people are part of Yousafzai's movement, people who she defines as activists and encourages to speak up—just as she does.

## BARACK OBAMA AND ROBERT F. KENNEDY BUILD GOLDEN BRIDGES

Obama was always the bridge candidate. In a country such as the United States, with groups long divided along racial lines, he was, in fact, the bridge himself. And he used this concept in his speeches. At the Democratic National Convention in 2004, he attempted to build a long list of bridges: "There's not a liberal America and a conservative America. There's the United States of America. There's not a black America and white America and Latino America and Asian America; there's the United States of America."

By early 2008, things looked a bit different. What had been a golden bridge was looking less solid and less appealing as Obama was confronted with statements from Jeremiah Wright, while running for president. Wright was Obama's local pastor and had officiated at his wedding to Michelle Obama. Wright had also inspired Barack Obama's 2006 memoir *The Audacity of Hope* and the keynote address mentioned above. Wright's statements were taken to justify terrorist attacks on the United States as a consequence of foreign wars and argued that the Founding Fathers, the writers of the Constitution and Declaration of Independence, lied when claiming that all men are created equal.

In response to Wright's comments, Obama made a speech called "A More Perfect Union," and it is, in my humble opinion, one of the best he ever gave. In it, he stated,

> I can no more disown him [Rev. Wright] than I can disown the black community. I can no more disown him than I can disown my white grandmother—a woman who helped raise me, a woman who sacrificed again and again for me, a woman who loves me as much as she loves anything in this world, but a woman who once confessed her fear of black men who passed her by on the street, and who on more than one occasion has uttered racial or ethnic stereotypes that made me cringe.
>
> These people are a part of me. And they are part of America, this country that I love.

Obama builds a bridge between Wright (and many Black Americans identifying with his statements) and his white grandmother (and those relating to her experiences). But he does not stop there. Four years later, Obama visited Ireland, where one part of his family hails from. It was spring as he landed in Dublin, and again he built a bridge while speaking from the lawn outside Dublin College:

> It was remarkable to see the small town where a young shoemaker named Falmouth Kearney, my great-great-great grandfather, my grandfather's grandfather, lived his early life. And I was shown the records from the parish recording his birth. And we saw the home where he lived.
>
> And he left during the Great Hunger, as so many Irish did, to seek a new life in the New World. He traveled by ship to New York, where he entered himself into the records as a laborer. He married an American girl from Ohio. They settled in the Midwest. They started a family.
>
> It's a familiar story because it's one lived and cherished by Americans of all backgrounds. It's integral to our national identity. It's who we are, a nation of immigrants from all around the world.

Obama builds golden bridges by using his own story as an asset and demonstrating how it relates to the lives of his audience. He bridges the gulfs between political persuasions, Black and white Americans, and across an ocean—the Atlantic—to Ireland. Through these connections, he aligns himself with his audience, enabling them to take in his message through the process of identification.

Where Obama used his family background to build bridges, Robert F. Kennedy used his tragic personal experiences. Let me take you back to the evening of April 4, 1968. Martin Luther King Jr. was murdered on a balcony at the Lorraine Motel in Memphis, Tennessee. At the same hour, Robert F. Kennedy was boarding a plane to Indianapolis, Indiana, for a rally as part of his presidential campaign against Richard Nixon. On board the

Robert F. Kennedy's speech following the assassination of Martin Luther King Jr. has been credited with keeping people calm in the wake of the tragedy.

plane he was told of King's assassination, and as he took the stand to deliver his speech, the crowd was unaware of King's death. Kennedy was wearing a jacket that belonged to his brother—President John F. Kennedy, who was shot and killed five years earlier in Dallas, Texas.

Robert F. Kennedy—without preparation—used his own public experience with death to build a bridge to his audience, to create a connection. He said, "For those of you who are black and are tempted to be filled with hatred and distrust at the injustice of such an act, against all white people, I can only say that I feel in my own heart the same kind of feeling. I had a member of my family killed, but he was killed by a white man. But we have to make an effort in the United States, we have to make an effort to understand, to go beyond these rather difficult times."

After the murder of Martin Luther King Jr., protests erupted in more than a hundred US cities. Twenty-five hundred people were wounded, and thirty-nine died in the violence. But Indianapolis did not experience the same levels of unrest as similar cities.

## HOW TO BUILD A GOLDEN BRIDGE

Action does follow from knowledge, but often it is the other way around. Our preexisting beliefs control how we perceive and interpret new knowledge. We evaluate the credibility of sources, interpret motives of messengers, and often downright reject information that does not fit our established opinions. Our opinions form around the values we have, and they are often a matter of group identification. This tendency is called confirmation bias, and it affects polarizing topics such as climate a lot. When the topic is heavy with scientific jargon, complicated calculations, long timelines, and global politics—as is the case with climate—it gets even worse. Our brains simply procrastinate reflecting on the new information if it does not fit the mold. This proves a problem when trying to persuade people who don't understand or believe in climate change. While it's possible that your audience might reflect on the information you provide them long after you have stopped talking, more likely they might not be able to do that due to confirmation bias, especially if all you do is convey information.

But there is a well-established way to do more than convey information, and that is to present yourself as someone worth listening to. You can do that by seeming interested in others, expressing empathy with your audience, identifying with the values of the people you seek to convince, and using metaphors that effectively translate your audience's values to your own. As we saw with the speech about the penguin family, storytelling is the best way to foster identification with your audience, so try to find a narrative that touches on their values.

Studies into effective climate communication have shown that there are three things to remember when speaking about climate so you can overcome the audience's confirmation bias:

1. **Share the values of your audience.** It is always important to adapt your message to your audience—even more so when the topic is abstract, controversial, and polarizing. Research shows that confirmation bias is put on hold when climate action is presented as a logical conclusion stemming from values shared by the audience. And there is no need to worry about losing climate allies. Allies will have no problem connecting climate action to their own values, regardless of what values you explicitly refer to.
2. **Emotional stories beat neutral information.** Speeches are not suitable for conveying neutral information, and as we saw in chapter 1, values and emotions are a central part of how we make decisions as human beings. Research has shown that neutral information is actually worse than not communicating at all. It is counterproductive because it increases polarization and in effect prevents the audience from listening to views that they disagree with. On the other hand, emotional stories use feelings instead of logic. The mechanism of confirmation bias is circumvented because emotions compel us to identify with a speaker. An easy way to tell an emotionally compelling story is to give detailed accounts of characters fighting obstacles to achieve their goals.

3. **Open-ended stories increase motivation for action.**
   Most likely, after appealing to the values of your audience and presenting your message in an emotionally compelling narrative, you want them to take action. To effectively motivate them, your story needs to be open-ended. People need a reason to act—the story cannot be over yet. That is one of the reasons that overoptimistic stories of heroes solving the climate crisis does not motivate action—the hero has already taken care of the problem. It is also one of the reasons that doomsday rhetoric—where everything will likely fail and we will all likely die—does not motivate action. Both increase polarization. We have to find an ending to the story somewhere in between, yet with a negative twist to make the case that there is something at stake.

In his book *The Political Brain*, psychologist Drew Westen writes that climate activists should refrain from using words such as *environment* and *climate* altogether. Instead, he recommends that we speak about what climate and environment mean to us—what values and emotions are associated with them. We have to be concrete and emotional when storytelling. Then we can bring up ideas that speak to the audience's particular values, such as protecting our homeland to pass it on to the next generation. Or we can talk about the clean air we breathe, the clean water we serve our kids to drink, the lakes and rivers we used to go fishing in, and the animals we used to see in nature. We can even talk about being stewards of creation. What is most important is that we actually feel it. It has to be our values, too, or it will seem (and be) false. Make the case for those shared values and demonstrate how they are threatened by the climate crisis.

Global warming is not just about science and numbers, it is

about all the stuff we love and are about to lose. We have to make it familiar to the people we want to affect, not just threatened species living in faraway lands or changes that will occur in a distant future. When on the podcast *Future of StoryTelling*, Gore said, "Wherever possible it helps to connect the climate issue to other concerns that people have, about their health for example, about their kids, the fate of places they deeply love."

Connect the climate to something your audience loves so you can build a golden bridge. You can do it by researching the audience beforehand, talking to members of that group (in person or on social media), and taking some time to think about what they would spend their time thinking and talking about. What are their key values, and what might connect emotionally? What experiences do you have in common? The most important thing is to remember that you are both human, which is a great place to start.

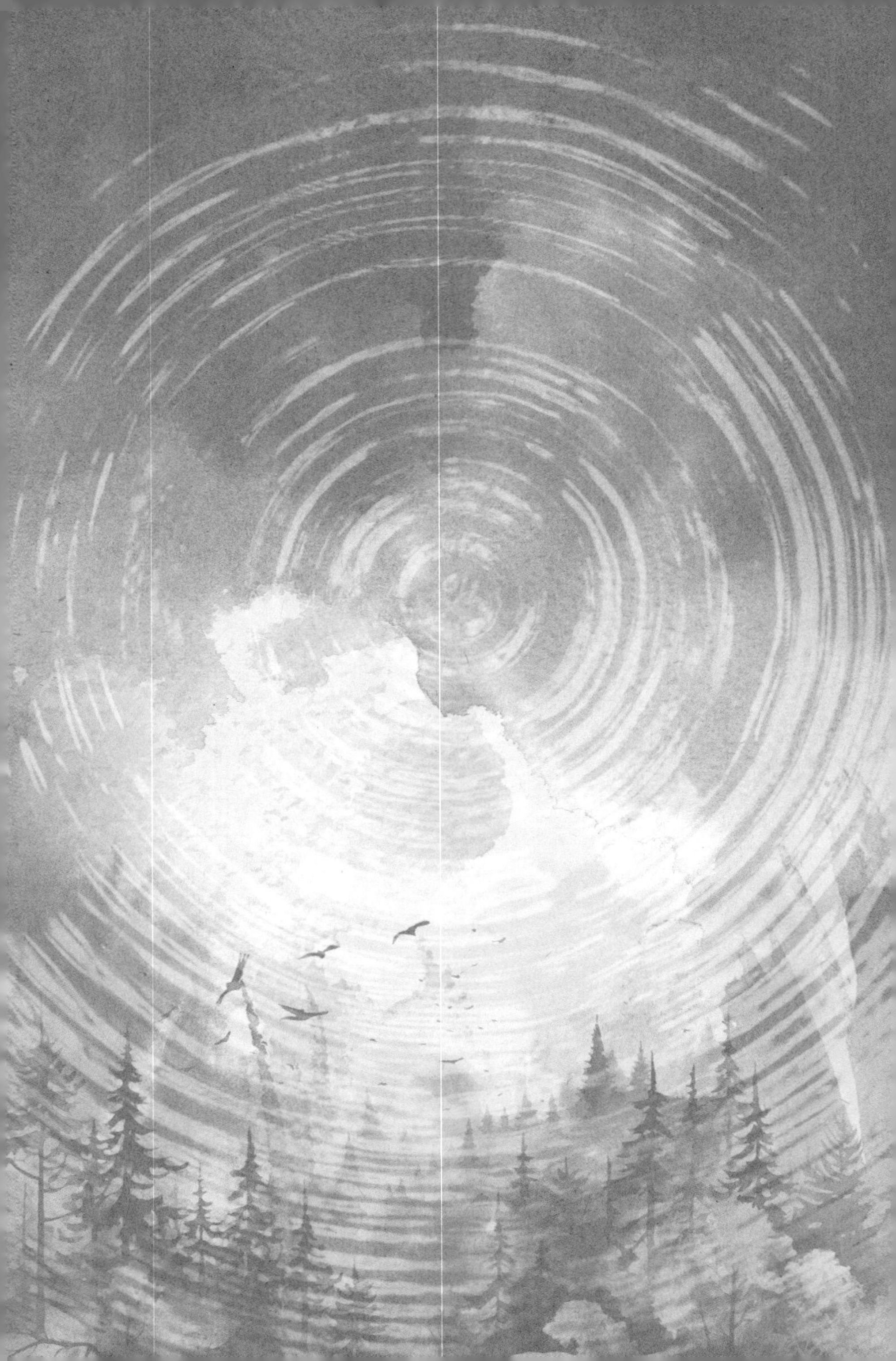

# CHAPTER 5
## TELL THE STORY OF YOUR JOURNEY

One day when I was writing speeches in the Danish Ministry for Climate, Energy and Buildings, I asked the minister to tell me the story about how he came to realize that climate was the most important issue. He said he had always known. And that was too bad. Because if you have always known what you are trying to communicate to others, then it becomes more difficult to persuade them. With a personal story about what he used to think, what convinced him, and what the world looks like now, he would have been able to persuade more people.

People tend to grow tired of listening to climate activists who talk as if they have always known what they know now and have never changed their minds. It sounds lofty and preachy. It ignores the common human experience of doubt and reflection—of change—and thus it does not invite the audience to change their minds. This principle applies regardless of whether it is attitude, behavior, or action we want to change.

To change a mind, we must first show that it is acceptable for minds to change. The best way to do that is to talk about a time you changed yours. A listener will be much more easily convinced by someone who has been convinced themselves. Someone who knows what it is like to be in the listener's shoes and who shares their values. That someone is a much more trustworthy source. Admitting you didn't always know what you know now is simply more realistic, more credible, and more human.

As Gore said in the podcast I mentioned in the last chapter: "When I have a so-called Aha-moment, I love to recreate that Aha-moment for others."

Creating a narrative out of your own journey is just that. The power of storytelling is that you put people in your shoes and offer them a glimpse of your world the way you see it. As we saw before, speeches gain their power from identification, and identification comes from the use of emotion and the expression of your worldview. But moving people also requires that you take them on a journey—and your own journey is by far the best at producing identification. That is why as speechwriters, we must be better at talking about our doubts, describing what we struggled with, and admitting what we are still grappling to fully understand. Our audience will then be more inclined to understand and make the same decisions we have made.

Al Gore continues to speak out about the climate. He gave a speech at the 2022 Climate COP27 in Sharm el-Sheikh, Egypt.

Start with where your realities and values overlap with those of your audience. Then tell the story about how you were moved, so you can move them. Science and faith won't do it alone, but spun into a story, they just might create the traction you want.

## MY STORY

In 2021 I was asked to give a speech at a local climate protest in connection with the municipal elections in Denmark. There I told the story about what made me engage in the climate issue. How I didn't really want to join this movement at first, but then something happened, and I realized I had to take action: I became a father. That change in my perspective made me turn my activism toward the environment. And if I could turn into a climate activist, then so could my audience. The speech started this way:

> In the spring of 2009, I became a dad for the first time. We were living in Copenhagen in a small apartment at the time. And I remember standing with my baby girl in my arms—she had not turned one year old yet—when COP15 started and protesters marched down the street below our window with chants and music. I thought: Now something will happen! Now we will do this! Now we will solve this crisis! But we did not. It was a tremendous disappointment. We could not solve big, abstract, and global challenges. Democracy did not work. That was what the world taught me and my baby girl that day.
>
> I became a dad again five years later. And while I was on paternity leave with my baby boy, the UN Sustainable Development Goals were signed in September 2015 in New York. I thought: NOW something will happen! All world leaders had signed it. This is great, it is good, things are moving in the right direction. And nothing really

happened. December that same year, the Paris Agreement was created. I was ecstatic, jumping up and down, dancing and yelling. It was big—now something would change. But it did not.

I told a story about disappointment, but I did not make it only doom and gloom. I also told the story of the fight to fix the hole in the ozone layer, finding inspiration in the past. And I spoke of concrete actions to take and asked the audience to make promises to one another that they would commit to these actions:

> We must promise each other something else, too. Because after the election comes another day. And many of us are good at complaining about politicians and their unkept promises. But if we go vote one day and then forget the next, then we are the ones not keeping our promises. We have to keep at it. We have to keep going. We have to remind politicians of their promises to us, their promises to our children, and we have to help them keep them. It is not always going to be easy to find solutions. But keep the pressure—democracy also happens in between elections. Join a political party. Participate in a citizen climate council. Show up to a city council meeting and show them that this is important.
>
> And we have to promise one another that the climate promise is not going to be like the rest of them. This is the promise that has to be kept. We have to show our children and the young people of the world that promises are meant to be kept and crises are meant to be solved. That democracy works.

# PUBLIC NARRATIVE

In chapter 3, I mentioned Marshall Ganz. His theory of public narrative is where the concept of the story of self has been popularized as a means for the mobilization of social movements. Public narrative describes how mobilizing for a candidate or a cause is about telling the right kind of stories. The right kind of story begins with describing the status quo, where everyone can recognize the world we all live in (building the golden bridge), and then presents a challenge or a call to action of some kind. The protagonist (most likely yourself and, by extension, your audience) faces a difficult choice between maintaining the status quo or making a significant life change. As the protagonist struggles to do the right thing, they encounter setbacks, challenges, and doubts, but eventually their decision leads to a better status quo than

Marshall Ganz (*center*) has helped many people organize to support a cause. Here he speaks to Occupy Boston in 2011.

before. The message of such a story is that when we rely on our values to make hard choices, those choices can lead us to a better future. And you will tell it best by using an example from your own life.

Ganz calls this narrative a story of self. In theorizing it, he draws on a long-established Jewish tradition dating back to Babylon. The rabbi Hillel the Elder was known for coining the ethics within the phrase: "If I am not for myself, who will be for me? And being only for myself, what am 'I'? And if not now, when?"

According to Ganz, your audience will need three questions answered if they are to follow you. These three questions, or stories, he calls story of self, story of us, and story of now.

## STORY OF SELF

Your audience might ask, Why should we listen to you? They will not be moved as a favor to you. They will only be moved for their own sake, and they are looking for something in return. They are looking for you to provide meaning, community, and a cause bigger than themselves and bigger than you. Your task is to inspire them to make hard decisions by appealing to their values and emotions and preparing them to know that it will not be easy. There is always a story about why we are where we are. That story contains a choice and an action, and it tells us something about being human that can inspire us to act accordingly.

## STORY OF US

Your audience will ask, How can we do this? Moving people means many things, and your audience consists of many different people from as many different lives and circumstances. They have a range of attitudes, experiences, and motivations. You have to unite them as "us" and show this group how your collective values and actions in the past have enabled change, as discussed in chapters 3 and 4. The important thing here is that you create an "us" with a tradition highlighting what values to draw from, what past to be inspired by, and what skills to employ—a tradition that should be extended from the past to the present.

## STORY OF NOW

Your audience will wonder, Why does it have to be now? We are asking people to make hard choices on urgent issues. It is only human to try to postpone making difficult decisions. That goes for politicians, company leadership, consumers, and potential activists. And it can be an incredibly frustrating experience to know the coming consequences of the climate crisis and the scale of what it demands of us, while seeing people around us postpone enacting solutions. That is why your speech should tell the audience why it's the right time to act and why we can't wait. Why it is a logical extension of their deepest values to act now. It can be hard to predict what hardships the audience will endure, but we should try to prepare them.

So far most of the climate conversation has been about urgency and now, now, now. But it has not worked. We have been trying to convince people to act on a global, emotionally impactful issue with science and graphs lacking emotion, values, and identification. When all you present are facts to an audience who disagrees with you, they are much more likely to double down on their preexisting beliefs.

A climate conversion should never be the goal of a speech or a conversation. Yet the story of your journey will serve both as a model of your experience and as a model for others to shape their experiences. This is what enables their conversion. A conversion in this regard can be from climate denier to climate action advocate, but it can also be to move people from inactive to active, or simply to increase the number of actions they are taking and deepen the commitment they have to addressing the issue.

Some of the best pieces of climate communication I have encountered have been from concerned scientists. In particular, I remember seeing a video clip of a biologist standing on the beach next to the Great Barrier Reef in Australia. She cried while talking about the reef she had studied her whole life, and how it was disappearing before she had a chance to show it to her daughter. Unfortunately, I don't remember where I saw it, and I don't remember who it was, but the message and the emotion stuck with me. The reef was one of the places she loved deeply, and it was in danger. It was easy to understand why she was the one to tell this story. It was highly emotional, and it presented a clear and understakable urgency—the story of self, us, and now. I tried to do the same thing with the story of the daddy penguin in chapter 1.

Coral bleaching occurs when warm water causes corals to expel the algae that live in them. Though coral can survive a bleaching event, such as the one seen here in the Great Barrier Reef, they are much more vulnerable to death.

Of course, your story might contain the science that convinced you, if it was indeed science that convinced you. But most people are motivated to change by a fear of losing something they cherish. Motivation can also come from thinking about the things they might gain by taking action, but positives in a hypothetical future often seem abstract, and some people will interpret the potential gains you present to them as losing what they have now, such as their car, their house, and their family. A new unknown future, even if presented in a positive light, can seem like losing a comfortable and familiar present. Instead, take advantage of the fear of loss by reminding your audience what's at stake. The fear of losing something that you value can be your favorite spot in nature, the lake where you went fishing as a child, or the countryside enjoyed with your grandparents. It has to be concrete, value-based, and emotional. These images go across political divides. And they serve to trigger concrete actions—it's easier to imagine what you could do to preserve a small, local area than trying to save the entire world.

By telling your story of self, you take your audience by the hand and show them the way. You create a model for their experiences. And you show them that you are not the enemy, or an expert, but rather a human like them who has changed their mind.

## BARACK OBAMA SPOKE ABOUT HIS PATH

It is a staple in political speechwriting that candidates tell a story of self to explain why they are the right candidate and thus deserve your vote. (Often, they put less energy into telling us who we are and why it has to be now.) Many have used Ganz's theory to present their own story as a metaphor for a larger story of the community they seek to lead. Barack Obama was a community organizer in Chicago, Illinois, before he became a politician, and he no doubt was exposed to the teachings of Ganz there. His speech at the

Democratic Convention in 2004 is often used as an example of Ganz's approach:

> Tonight is a particular honor for me because, let's face it, my presence on this stage is pretty unlikely. My father was a foreign student, born and raised in a small village in Kenya. He grew up herding goats, went to school in a tin-roof shack. His father, my grandfather, was a cook, a domestic servant.
>
> But my grandfather had larger dreams for his son. Through hard work and perseverance my father got a scholarship to study in a magical place: America, which stood as a beacon of freedom and opportunity to so many who had come before. While studying here, my father met my mother. She was born in a town on the other side of the world, in Kansas. Her father worked on oil rigs and farms through most of the Depression. The day after Pearl Harbor he signed up for duty, joined Patton's army and marched across Europe. Back home, my grandmother raised their baby and went to work on a bomber assembly line.
>
> After the war, they studied on the G.I. Bill, bought a house through FHA, and moved west in search of opportunity.
>
> And they, too, had big dreams for their daughter, a common dream, born of two continents. My parents shared not only an improbable love; they shared an abiding faith in the possibilities of this nation. They would give me an African name, Barack, or "blessed," believing that in a tolerant America your name is no barrier to success. They imagined me going to the best schools in the land, even though they weren't rich,

because in a generous America you don't have to be rich to achieve your potential. They have both passed away now. Yet, I know that, on this night, they look down on me with pride.

Obama crafts a clear story of self and links it to a story of us. Only at the end comes a story of now urging people to vote—for then presidential candidate John Kerry. The three stories in his speech might have been better connected had he spoken in favor of himself. His personal life story aligns with the story he wants to tell about America and its values, and he presents himself as a symbol of this unity. If America is in a state of racial conflict, then Obama is the solution. That might be why many read the speech as the launch of his own future candidacy for US president—something that happened years later.

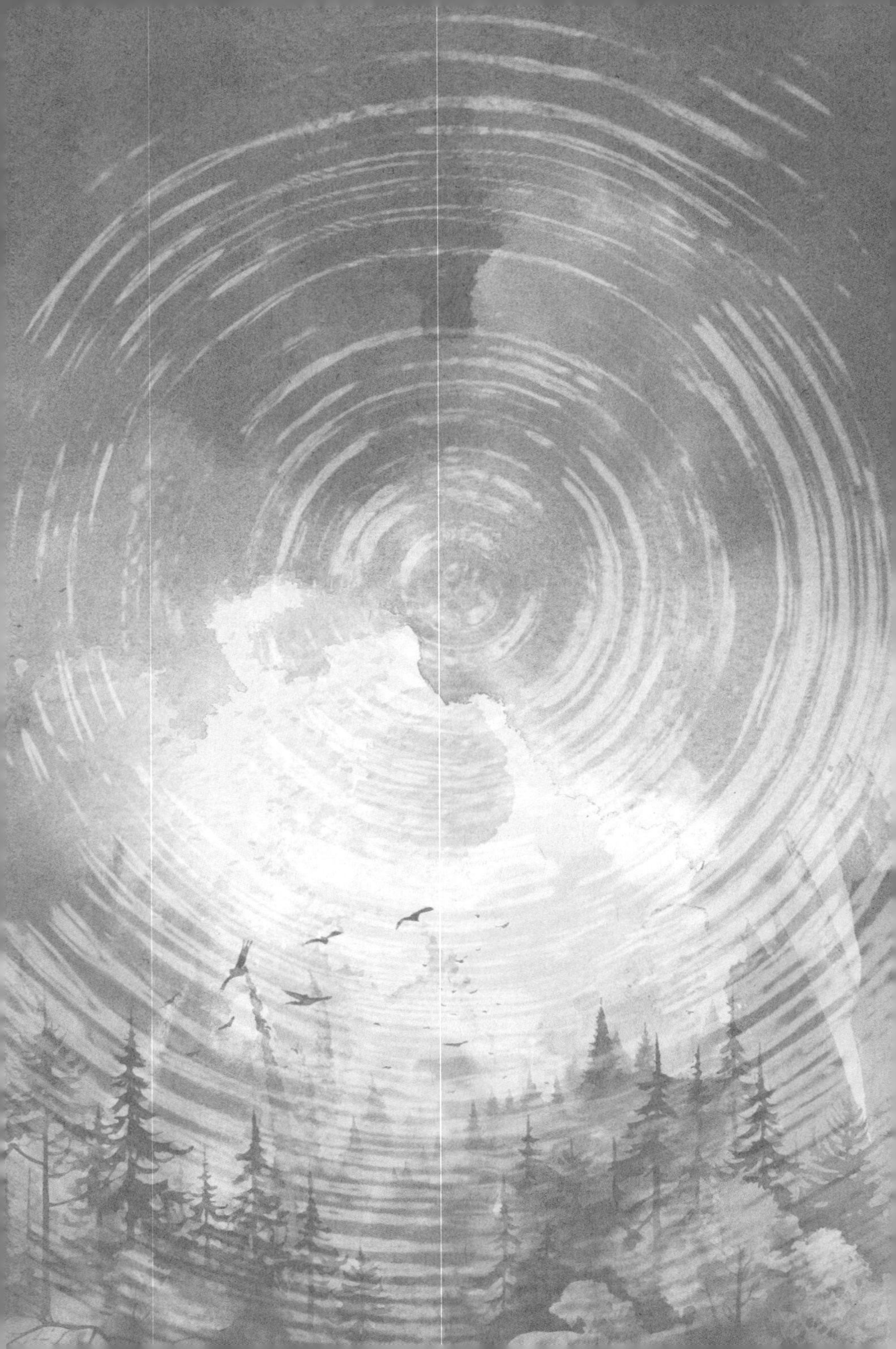

# CHAPTER 6
## CREATE COMMITMENT FOR CHANGE

In 2004 I took a Communication for Social Change course at Roskilde University in Denmark with the famous professor and expert on the topic Thomas Tufte. One thing that stuck with me from the course is the South African story of *Soul City*, and the change it caused.

*Soul City* was a forty-five-episode radio drama aired in nine languages starting in 1999. It took up different social challenges and themes and was very popular among poor villagers, who would gather around the radio to listen while imagining that they were part of a much wider audience of groups listening in other villages.

One of the challenges taken up in the show was domestic violence against women. There are several ways to treat this topic, such as informing the audience about how it affects people and how prevalent it is, describing the laws prohibiting it and how to seek medical help after experiencing it, or preparing women by talking about the red flags leading up to the violence. But the show did not do any of those. Because it was a show with a continuous storyline and a recurring cast of characters, it told a fictional story to make an emotional appeal.

At the time, it was socially accepted that domestic violence happened and was a private matter concerning only the family. Others would refrain from bringing it up, even if they heard it or could see the injuries afterward. When domestic violence happened in the village, people would make it a matter of household privacy and not intervene. The *Soul City* episode started by describing a situation like this, one that the audience could identify with. But instead of ignoring the situation, the characters gathered at the house, protested the violence, and intervened to throw out the aggressor and protect the victim. They acted contrary to the social norm.

After the episode aired, reports started to emerge that reality had imitated art. In some villages where domestic violence occurred, people had imitated the story from the radio. They had gathered, thrown out the aggressor, and protected the victim. The radio show story had changed what people expected from one another. They created a sense of community and changed the status quo.

A sense of community is created when each person in an audience—whether for a radio show or a speech—becomes aware that they are in a group, listening together, and begins imagining that the others in the group are listening to the same words and interpreting the same messages. They start looking for clues on how to react and adjust their own reactions accordingly, so as to remain part of the group. This is similar to the sense of community one can get when listening to the State of the Union address or when watching a game or favorite TV show. When you know that you are part of a group receiving the same messages, you start to feel a sense of identity, a sense of belonging, and that you have something in common with the other members of the group.

We can take advantage of this phenomenon to move our audiences toward a shared goal. We can convince our audience to commit to change together. By speaking out more and more, we can build a stronger sense of community and increase the social pressure to join, thus changing the status quo. By using humans' innate herd mentality and building a sense of community step by step, we can challenge and change the dominant story about climate and our relationship with the natural world.

## CHANGING THE DOMINANT NARRATIVE

Stories that are so commonly understood by a community that they need no explanation are called dominant narratives. Dominant narratives vary from culture to culture and evolve over time as cultural norms shift. Other stories might be popular in certain groups, but they will need explanations to be valid in other groups or at other times.

The dominant narrative about climate action is that it is much too expensive. The focus of the story is on the economics involved in taking action. As a result, investments in clean energy need explaining but exploitation of natural resources does not. Protecting habitats needs explaining, but drilling for oil does not. The price of inaction and the planetary impacts are disregarded. To get climate action at the scale and pace needed, we must push the climate action story to be the dominant narrative—the story we expect to happen.

Every time we tell the story of necessary climate action we strengthen that narrative. Every time we create a sense of community around needed climate action, we push that narrative. Every time we shift the burden of explanation, we push the norm and challenge the dominant narrative.

You can't do that alone, but the good news is you don't have to. Just as you might be frustrated with the lack of climate action, so might people in your audience. To be inspired to act, they need you to confirm their beliefs about needed climate action. Recent research has showed that about two-thirds of young people are extremely concerned about climate change, and about two-thirds never talk about it with anyone. That means, in the best of worlds, that one-third of young people feel as though they are carrying the fate of the world on their shoulders, all alone. Don't let them down if you have an opportunity to speak up.

When acknowledging that we help others reshape the story of how they see the world by sharing our own stories, we are moving into the terrain of narrative psychology. According to this approach, our identities are maintained through the retelling of stories about ourselves and our worldview, and psychological challenges arise when our stories are not accepted but need defending and explaining.

The good thing is that when we speak up, we redefine what is dominant. When our audience accepts a story, we tell them without us having to justify ourselves, we craft new stories for ourselves and that audience and enable new futures. It is one thing to have a story in your heart, but when it comes out and is validated through a collective group dynamic, it can change the world. This is one way to help people out of feelings of isolation, fear, and anxiety about the climate crisis. It is the path toward action and community, by changing expectations.

## MANDELA USES HIS STORY TO CREATE COMMITMENT

Most people know Nelson Mandela, the man who became the symbol of the peaceful struggle against South African apartheid. But he is part of a larger story. In the 1600s Dutch and British merchants established colonies and trading outposts in the land that became South Africa and eventually established the country across the existing borders of different tribes' territories. South Africa's history was full of conflicts between a small, rich, and European elite and the poor African majority, but it was not until after the Second World War that the white National Party took power. With inspiration from Adolf Hitler, they established the apartheid laws mandating racial segregation, outlawing interracial marriage, and registering all South Africans as either white, Black, or colored. This led to protests and civil disobedience from the African National Congress (ANC)—led by Nelson Mandela, one of the founders of the youth branch of the organization in 1944.

In 1960 the ANC was made illegal, leading Mandela to form and lead a paramilitary group, uMkhonto weSizwe (Spear of the Nation), to sabotage the government. The organization and its activities were also illegal, and despite operating in secret, in August 1962, he was arrested and jailed. He stood trial along with other ANC members in 1964, and the courtroom battle started with Nelson Mandela's speech.

Mandela was convinced that he would be executed no matter what he said and decided that he might as well say what he thought. He intended to explain the rationale behind the actions of the ANC, its politics, and its values. While conflicts were escalating within the country, the apartheid system in South Africa had drawn international concern. The United Nations had urged countries to enact an embargo against South Africa, and South Africa was excluded from the Olympics Committee in 1970. Aware of the growing attention on his case, Mandela directed the speech toward a wider audience than that in the courtroom.

Awaiting the trial in jail, he prepared his remarks. For weeks he worked on the speech and had it approved by his friends. But his lawyers argued against it. They thought sections were too uncompromising and would damage the case, possibly leading to conviction. So Mandela added "if needs be" in the last sentence. The speech lasted three hours and the controversial sections—and the added sentence—were the very last. The last part also stood out as Mandela turned to face the judge and looked him straight in the eye. This is what he said: "During my lifetime I have dedicated myself to this struggle of the African people. I have fought against white domination, and I have fought against black domination. I have cherished the ideal of a democratic and free society in which all persons live together in harmony and with equal opportunities. It is an ideal which I hope to live for and to achieve. But if needs be, it is an ideal for which I am prepared to die."

In the courtroom, Mandela lost. The group was sentenced to life in prison. But outside the courtroom, Mandela became a symbol of progress. In 1989 then South African president F. W. de Klerk agreed to meet Mandela. He then began the process of abolishing the racial segregation policies in public spaces and started releasing imprisoned ANC members. In 1990 the ANC was legalized again, and Mandela was released from prison. De Klerk removed the last of the apartheid laws, and then the United Nations' international sanctions were removed. In 1993 South Africa ratified a new constitution, and de Klerk and Mandela won the Nobel Peace Prize together. The year after, Mandela was elected president—in the first election he was allowed to vote in. South Africa was also reinstated in the United Nations.

But back to his speech. When Mandela stepped out of prison, his first words to the gathered reporters were identical to those he delivered in the courtroom before going to prison twenty-seven years earlier. The words above, the same ones that launched him into international fame and drew attention to the struggle to end apartheid. But why had they become so influential?

The answer is they were a commitment to an ideal. Mandela declared he would live or die for that ideal, which challenged his audience to do the same. When identifying with him they had to ask themselves: Can I commit to this ideal? Or are my ideals just for show? Would I—as Mandela did—commit to twenty-seven years in prison for my ideals?

Nelson Mandela (*center left*) was greeted by his wife, Winnie (*center right*), and a crowd of supporters upon his release from prison on February 11, 1990.

The speeches—before and after prison—were published in newspapers and heard on TV and radio. The audience, those who agreed with Mandela's cause, formed a sense of community that created an expectation. As a result, people were at risk of feeling like hypocrites and feared being confronted with that by others. So they committed. In 1994, four years after his release from prison, Mandela was elected president in South Africa's first fully democratic national elections, where all citizens, regardless of race, could vote. The ANC won a decisive victory, securing over half of the vote, which effectively marked the end of apartheid in South Africa.

## ÞORGEIR COMMITTED PEOPLE TO CHANGE

We are not the first generation to face rapid and all-encompassing transitions, nor the first to argue for that transition or for committing others to it. On a warm summer's day in the year 1000, people had gathered—some having traveled for several weeks—at Iceland's Þingvellir to make a decision about the fate of their country. It would be a battle between faiths and creeds, with weapons ready and lives on the line.

Would Iceland be pagan or Christian?

For generations, Iceland had been pagan, but times were changing in continental Europe, and more regions had converted to Christianity. Christian kings in Denmark and Norway were putting the pressure on their allies in Iceland to convert. So there they were: Pagans believing in the Nordic gods Thor, Odin, and Frey in one camp and Christians in another. Each side had their weapons ready in case of war. Emotions were high, and words and insults flew back and forth. A battle was just about to break out when someone yelled, "The Hengill volcano is erupting!" The Hengill volcano was just 10 miles (16 km) away.

Everyone stopped. Volcanic eruptions happened regularly on Iceland, but they were still dangerous, even deadly. Each side understood volcanic eruptions as an ill omen, either a symptom of gods fighting giants or the coming end of the world. The pagans had set up an altar beneath the volcano and made regular sacrifices in an attempt to maintain stability and appease the gods. But now they feared a tipping point had been reached. The eruption deepened the sense of unease and became a symbol of the growing tension and conflict.

The task of uniting the people fell on a man named Þorgeir Þorkelsson. He was a goði or pagan priest, but Þorgeir was widely respected as a lawspeaker across the island. He had to commit everybody in the country to respect the same laws, and he had to communicate his solution in a way that mobilized everybody. If he was not successful, a religious civil war could break out, perhaps lasting for generations. Þorgeir contemplated what to do. The atmosphere was ripe with tension. Finally, after twenty-four hours, Þorgeir stepped out of his tent and summoned everybody to Law Rock—where laws were proposed and agreed upon.

Þorgeir started by asking people to swear that they respect and keep the law he was about to propose. The Icelandic sagas are not in total agreement about what he said, but this is a translated version (my translation from Danish):

I believe that immense damage will happen if people do not follow the same law and one faith in this country. If the law is split, the peace will be too, and misunderstandings and discord will escalate to animosity, unrest, and war. If we do not proceed wisely we may wreck our country. We must do everything we can to avoid a civil war in this country. Let us strive for agreement and peace in our country.

Did you not hear how the kings of Norway and Denmark were at war with each other so long that the chiefs in both countries grew tired and made an agreement and peace against the will of the kings? But that settlement led to the kings also making peace. Even though our chiefs are not as mighty as the kings of other countries, and we are not as wise as their counselors, we would be wise to follow their example.

And it seems advisable to me not to let those who oppose each other here with most vehemence prevail, and instead let us arbitrate between them so that each side has its own way in something, but we all have the same law and the same religion, because this will prove true: if we tear apart the law, then we tear apart the peace.

Therefore: My advice is that we keep the peace and remove any cause for disagreement.

Þorgeir sat down. Everybody applauded and stated their support for Þorgeir's law. And then he spoke again: "The start of this law is that all people on Iceland—big and small—must be Christian. Those who are not baptized must become baptized. All pagan temples and godly figures must be destroyed."

He went on to explain how some pagan customs would still be allowed, as long as people were discreet about performing them, and that other laws not pertaining to religion still applied.

Although this is a translation of an ancient epic poem, we can still analyze the structure of Þorgeir's argument. As in most poetry of the time, there was a lot of alliteration but also repetition of the message that peace means upholding a common law based on a common religion. It is a very secular and modern argument elevating the peace of society over the salvation of individual souls.

The structure of Þorgeir's speech and the strength of his argument is central to how he commits people to accept a tremendous change in their lives and country.

- He starts by presenting his core argument—peace in Iceland means one law and one faith.
- He describes two scenarios and the future each will bring—civil war or peace.
- He demonstrates how bad it can be with known examples the audience can identify with—Denmark and Norway.
- He urges unity and compromise to achieve commitment.
- He presents his solution but softens it with exceptions.

Using this structure Þorgeir convinced his audience to commit to a radical change. They already agreed to respect his ruling beforehand, and they stated so publicly. If anybody was to disrespect the ruling and the law now it would mean that they had abandoned their word and their honor. They would be a hypocrite, having broken their oath—a serious offense in 1000 CE Iceland. But by including exceptions, Þorgeir also gave room for people to resist without breaking the law, without breaking their oath.

Þorgeir's speech worked. Iceland became Christian and avoided large-scale conflict, human sacrifice, and civil war.

## HERD MENTALITY AND COMMITMENT

Humans are a herd. In crowds, we tend to go where the people around us go. We follow. And we try to live up to the expectations of others as we understand them. This often results in a reluctance to change the status quo, because it means going against what we perceive as the majority position. In the case of the climate crisis, this phenomenon creates opposition to transitioning away from fossil fuels and other radical, large-scale changes. But it does not have to be like that. We can learn how to make people commit to change by taking advantage of the subconscious group dynamics that emerge when those people gather to listen to a speech. Behavioral economists Richard H. Thaler and Cass R. Sunstein describe how to do this through a concept they call "nudging," or "affecting the context in which people make decisions to improve those decisions by using cognitive biases and not rational choices."

Pushing for change means challenging the status quo. And within nudging, there are quite a few concepts that can prove useful in making that change possible and even plausible. For instance, research has demonstrated that the fear of loss is twice as powerful in influencing decision-making as the eagerness for gain. To take advantage of this psychological phenomenon, the change you advocate for should be framed as prevention of loss, not as a gain.

People react stronger to the risk of losing what they value than the chance of winning a bright new future.

In 1921 economist John Maynard Keynes noticed something strange in how people made choices: they overwhelmingly preferred options with known risks over options with unknown ones, even if those unknown risks are less significant. This might be called "the devil you know beats the devil you don't," but it was scientifically popularized as the Ellsberg paradox. And we prefer options where we have a chance to affect the outcome. This is even stronger when people feel they have been left without actionable choices, or when social norms are at play. Your speech should present climate action as the option with fewer known risks and inaction as carrying many unknown risks.

Finally, try to get your audience to commit to a concrete action. If they commit to something, it shifts from being something they potentially gain to something they could lose. Just like the audience listening to Þorgeir's speech, people fear losing the link between values and actions—being a hypocrite—a fear that is amplified in a collective context. The little voice in the back of your head is one thing, but the fear of people confronting you about the gulf between your values and your actions is quite another. The feeling or knowledge that you are being hypocritical is called cognitive dissonance. As humans, we strive to create order and consistency between our behavior/actions and our values/principles, so we try to avoid cognitive dissonance.

The status quo also comprises routines: going about your day without reflecting on what you do. Routines are easy and mindless. In contrast, change is hard. It launches you into the unknown, necessitating a lot of active choices. Changing might exclude you from whatever group you see yourself as part of, especially with regard to such a polarizing topic as climate. You might even have conflicts with friends, family, or colleagues. But by demonstrating how climate action is closely linked to your community's values, you can begin to challenge the status quo. Conversations with people who disagree with you will become easier when you start from what you have in common. Once you make that connection, that's when you explain how the change you advocate for will help the audience avoid losing what they value.

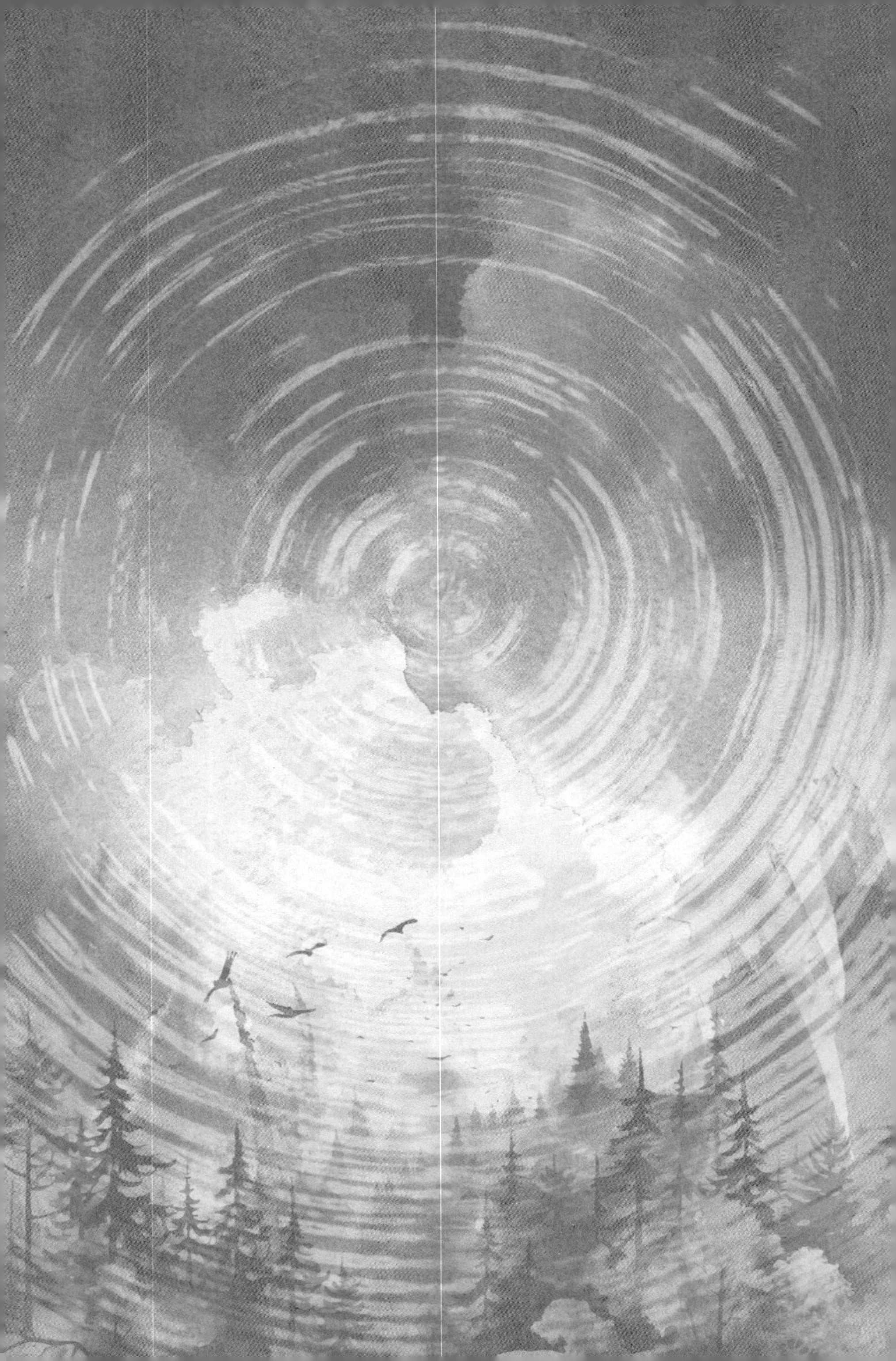

# CHAPTER 7
# USE THE ONE RING

Do not tell your audience all they need to know; tell them the one thing they need to remember.

Humans do not have the same capacity to retain information as goldfish. According to some research, we actually have a shorter attention span. We rarely remember something for long, we tend to adapt it to what we are currently focused on, and we rarely remember more than one thing. That is why your speech must refrain from telling your audience every detail you think they should know and focus on one thing they must remember long term. For every nonessential thing you tell your audience, you risk them remembering that over more vital information. That is one of the key insights of all experienced speechwriters: Tell them the most important thing. Repeat it and say it in many different ways. The audience might be distracted, a phone might ring, they might have an itch, or they might hear a noise. So you never know what part of the speech they will remember.

Repeat, repeat, repeat. Doesn't that make for a dull speech? It can. But repetition of a message is not the same as duplication of words. You should plan to repeat as a refrain in a song, not as a broken record. And there are many ways to make the same argument and deliver the same message. Using them reduces the risk of the audience remembering the wrong message, but it also has the advantage of differentiating and thus targeting different parts of the audience. Some might remember the refrain; others will remember the wordplay, the way you made them feel, or the metaphor. Still others will recall the story you told, and some might be more visual and remember the prop you used. But they should all point back to the same thing—your message.

## THE DREAM OR THE BROKEN PROMISE?

Whenever you speak about speeches, someone will bring up Martin Luther King Jr.'s "I Have a Dream" speech from 1963. It is arguably one of the best speeches in history, or as I would argue, two of the best speeches. Yet we only remember it as one, and I fear that King would not be happy if he knew the one that we remember.

The story goes that on the eve of the March on Washington in 1963, King was sitting with his friends and advisers in the lobby of the Willard Hotel discussing the speech for the next day. He asked if he should include the "I have a dream" portion, but they all agreed not to. It had been used in sermons and at marches for quite a while. It had become cliché, and it did not fit the occasion, as the aim was more real change and less dreaming. It did not have the confrontational associations they wanted. So the "dream" did not make it into the speech that night; it also was not in the script when King stopped revising and went to bed at 4 a.m., and it was not in his notes when he woke up or when he stepped to the podium the day after. He intended to give a very different speech to the crowd in emotion (impatience, confrontation, injustice) and metaphor (broken promises, bankrupt bank of justice, promissory note).

His speech was about broken promises and the historic struggle against enslavement and injustice. He spoke about how the Emancipation Proclamation was "a great beacon of hope" for Black Americans, yet a hundred years after, Black people were still not

More than two hundred thousand people gathered in Washington, DC, for the March on Washington for Jobs and Freedom when Martin Luther King Jr. delivered his famous speech.

free. He spoke about a check, a "promissory note," and a promise of freedom, equality, and justice—and how America had defaulted on that promise. He spoke about "the fierce urgency of now," and how now was not the time to relax and compromise on freedom. According to King, it was a time for action, and he announced that "the whirlwind of revolt will continue to shake the very foundations of our nation until the bright day of justice emerges." He said nothing about dreaming.

Then he spoke about how the road to freedom and equality should remain nonviolent and not divide people. That the struggle should continue as long as there was police brutality, racial segregation, and limits on the right to vote. He recognized the participants in the audience have struggled and felt the consequences of returning from prison cells and recovering from acts of violence. And he asked them to bring their struggles back to their home states and continue to fight for change. The speech was confrontational, action-oriented, and focused on broken promises. Just as he had agreed with his advisers the day before, with no mention of a dream.

It was a very good speech. It was well structured and thought through so that the elements strengthened one another, and the metaphors naturally progressed. King was an excellent speaker, and he delivered the speech very close to what was written. But something happened then that he did not intend. From behind him, gospel singer Mahalia Jackson yelled, "Tell them about the dream, Martin!" So King—for unknown reasons—started giving a very different second speech.

The "I Have a Dream" speech came to define him and all that he had done up to that point. It was with those words that he was later received by then president John F. Kennedy at the White House shortly after. But then nothing happened. Silence. The intention of the speech was to spur action, but it was not mentioned in the political work leading up to the Civil Rights Act in 1964. It seemed the political establishment did not want to associate itself with the confrontational rhetoric of the first speech, and the Civil Rights Movement was too impatient to embrace the utopian dream of the second speech.

It took five years and the murder of King for the speech to gain popularity in 1968. And it was not the whole of what King said that day that was recognized. Focus had now shifted to the second speech, and what was intended to be the "Broken Promises" speech had effectively become the "I Have a Dream" speech. People remembered "the table of brotherhood," yet forgot "the whirlwind of revolt." I feel confident that King would not have been satisfied with that.

The "I Have a Dream" speech is a reminder that speeches can be appropriated years after they are given, and what is remembered might not be as intended. King was not the only one.

## ANOTHER SHINING CITY UPON A HILL

On March 21, 1630, John Winthrop was preaching to his congregation at a church in Holyrood in Southampton, England. A large part of the congregation decided soon after to migrate to Massachusetts, New England, on board the ship *Arabella*. We have no way of knowing exactly what they thought of that particular sermon. We only know that Winthrop brought it with him, and it lay hidden for about two hundred years until it resurfaced and was published in 1882 by the Massachusetts Historical Society. Since then, its imagery has become a staple of US political rhetoric. The sermon notes read, "For we must consider that we shall be as a city upon a hill. The eyes of all people are upon us."

His metaphor of "a city upon a hill" has been quoted by presidents including John F. Kennedy, Ronald Reagan, and Barack Obama, as well as other politicians including Mitt Romney and Ted Cruz. The words have become part of so-called civil religion and synonymous with

John Winthrop was the first governor of the Massachusetts Bay Colony and was reelected to the post twelve times.

American exceptionalism. But there is a twist. It seems that nobody heard the rest of Winthrop's speech.

When reading the full sermon, Winthrop's message was that the pilgrims had a duty to act as though they were "a city upon a hill," or God would leave them, and they would be forgotten by history. The sentence after the quote above reads, "So that if we shall deal falsely with our God in this work we have undertaken, and so cause Him to withdraw His present help from us, we shall be made a story and a byword through the world."

Winthrop's message was one of acting morally so as to deserve God's grace, yet it was turned on its head to argue that the grace of God proved the morality of people's actions. The image, or metaphor, was taken out of context, and Winthrop's warning later in the sermon was conveniently forgotten: "But if our hearts shall turn away, so that we will not obey, but shall be seduced, and worship other Gods, our pleasure and profits, and serve them; it is propounded unto us this day, we shall surely perish out of the good land whither we pass over this vast sea to possess it."

Martin Luther King Jr.'s "Broken Promises" was overshadowed by "I Have a Dream," and John Winthrop's moral words were overshadowed by their cautionary intention. This misremembering of the message can happen fast, and it can happen to you too. Ensure that you have only one message and that it is thoroughly integrated into every element of your speech, so that no matter what part of your words they remember, they remember your message.

## THE ONE RING METHOD

To be certain that your message is what the audience receives no matter which part of the speech they remember, you can use the One Ring method. It is designed to reduce the risk of the audience remembering the wrong part of the speech or attributing the wrong meaning to your words.

## HOW TO USE THE ONE RING METHOD
**Identify your message, and write it in the middle of a piece of paper.**
   The message should be what you want people to remember afterward. I usually try to imagine this scenario: Two friends are planning to attend my speech. Let's call them Ann and George. Ann is in the audience, yet George gets a flat tire on the way there and only arrives right after the speech is done. As he arrives, he asks Ann, "What did he say?" The speech's message is that one sentence that Ann says to George right before they leave and get distracted by life.
   It can be, "We CAN solve the climate crisis!" "We really should start voting according to climate action," "We are doomed," "Planting trees is the way to go," or "We have to revolt against the system." Regardless of what the message is, you need to make sure your speech communicates it clearly and memorably, or else what Ann says to George won't reflect your intentions.

**Draw a ring around your message on the paper.**
   This is the One Ring. In drafting your speech, you will use several elements to drive home the message in the ring. The One Ring method consists of a refrain, a wordplay, an emotion, a metaphor, a story, and a prop, but you might use other elements as well. The idea is to write each of the elements in a circle around the main message. Because people might remember only one of the elements, the One Ring should ensure that each is integrated and connected. The ring is only as strong as the weakest link, so the elements should strengthen one another. Insert ideas for the above as part of the ring, and adapt to make them logically connected.

*REFRAIN • WORDPLAY • EMOTION*

*YOUR MESSAGE*

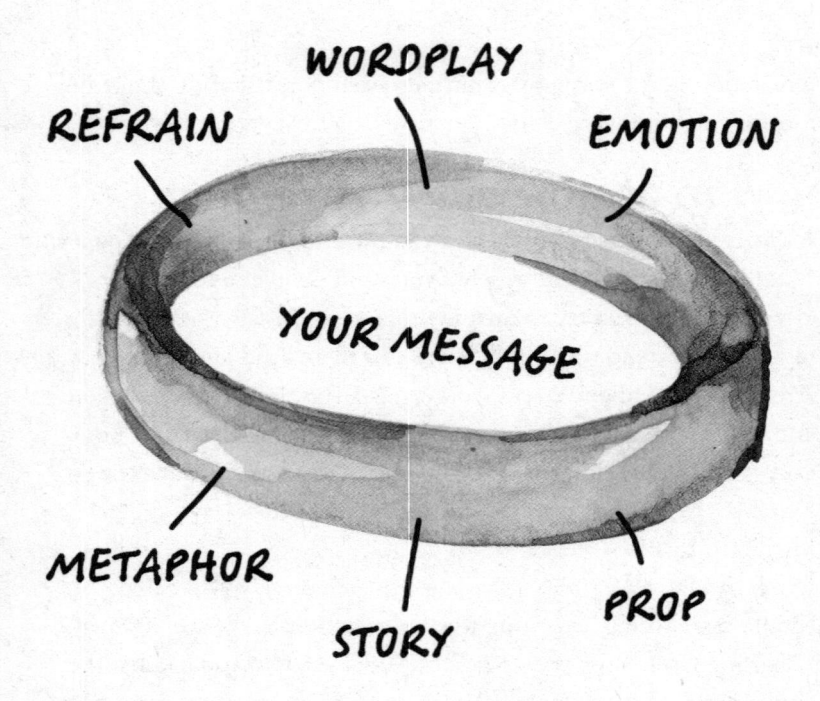

*METAPHOR • STORY • PROP*

## REFRAIN

A good refrain captures your message and makes it appealing, like the refrain in a catchy song. It should be short and suitable for different contexts. It should stick close to the message as written in the middle of the ring. The refrain will be repeated throughout the speech to ensure that you do not fall victim to the fate of the "I Have a Dream" or the "city upon a hill" speeches.

Winston Churchill was a celebrated speaker and rhetorician. His three speeches leading up to the United Kingdom entering World War II are often mentioned in the top ten of speeches through history, with sound bites such as "we shall fight on the beaches," "band of brothers," and "our finest hour." His use of the refrain "we shall fight" is a case to study. Here is what he said in the speech on June 4, 1940:

Even though large tracts of Europe and many old and famous States have fallen or may fall into the grip of the Gestapo and all the odious apparatus of Nazi rule, we shall not flag or fail. We shall go on to the end. We shall fight in France, we shall fight on the seas and oceans, we shall fight with growing confidence and growing strength in the air, we shall defend our island, whatever the cost may be. We shall fight on the beaches, we shall fight on the landing grounds, we shall fight in the fields and in the streets, we shall fight in the hills; we shall never surrender.

Churchill wrote books about his experiences, including speechmaking, and books have been written about his speeches. Some even claim that he gave voice to the British people, giving them courage and inspiring them to do their part to win the war. Yet historian and author Richard Toye has found something more nuanced. At the time of the speech, Churchill's popularity was mixed, and nobody knew how the war would end. Just because the speeches came before the Allied forces won the war does not mean that they won the war because of the speeches. Using analysis of diaries and opinion polls from that time, Toye argues that this impression of Churchill's leadership exists in hindsight more than it did at the time of his speeches. We remember the refrain because it made Churchill's message clear—Britain would fight everywhere—and thus we remember the myth of Churchill as inspiring the British people to do their part to win the war.

## WORDPLAY

Wordplays of different types have many names, such as puns, metaphors, and rhymes. The essence of wordplay is to condense a message in a way that is short, inspiring, and memorable. People tend to remember plays on words better than ordinary sentences. President John F. Kennedy—and his speechwriter Ted Sorensen—were better at it than most. Here are three examples:

"Ask not what your country can do for you; ask what you can do for your country."

"The one unchangeable certainty is that nothing is unchangeable or certain."

"Let us never negotiate out of fear but let us never fear to negotiate."

Following the murder of Kennedy on November 22, 1963, First Lady Jacqueline Kennedy did not want the world to forget his legacy. Quoting the musical *Camelot*, she used a play on words to make her case. It is emotional and almost like a song: "'Don't let it be forgot, that once there was a spot, for one brief, shining moment that was known as Camelot.' . . . There'll be great presidents again . . . but there will never be another Camelot."

Notice how it rhymes (forgot, spot, Camelot). It includes references to heroic, nation-building adventure and myth (King Arthur). And she uses the past to insert meaning into the present and thus shape the future. With these elements, she creates poetry and nostalgia, instilling the feeling that something magical is gone forever.

## EMOTION

Jacqueline Kennedy chose nostalgia. You also have to choose an emotion that fits your message. And it has to carry all the way through. Greta Thunberg hit the headlines with her speech to the United Nations in 2019. It didn't have a refrain, but the emotion is unmistakable: her face, her tone, and every bit of her words were tense with anger. It was even coined the "How Dare You" speech because of how clear her fury was. You might not agree with her, but there was no mistaking what emotion she wanted to convey.

She might have angered some people, and the climate crisis is by no means solved, but the message was remembered afterward.

Speeches can also calm people down. Franklin D. Roosevelt became US president in 1933 with a looming bank crisis on the horizon. Roosevelt wanted to reestablish trust in the banks through his leadership, and he used speeches—or, as he called them, chats—to do it. His first fireside chat was broadcast over the radio and into people's homes. These speeches were not remembered for subtle rhetorical devices but for their use of soothing emotions. And the cracking fire behind him no doubt helped.

The chats were meant to calm people down and encourage them to redeposit their money in their bank accounts, thus reducing the bank crisis. And it worked. After hearing the speeches, citizens would write back letters to Roosevelt about their regained trust in the banking sector. The looming bank collapse was averted. All because Roosevelt created one emotion with his chats—calm.

## METAPHOR

British political speechwriter guru Simon Lancaster once remarked, "Metaphors are the nuclear weapon of communication." He asserts that they have the power to justify war, death, and climate action. That is why you must decide between Bush's noncommittal "climate change," Thunberg's "climate emergency," Gore's "climate crisis," Biden's "existential threat," or UN secretary general Guterres's "global boiling." Or one of your own making. Each one is a metaphor providing your audience with a quick way to understand your message by alluding to specific imagery and story.

At a conference about biodiversity in Trondheim, Norway, in 2004, former prime minister of Norway and later special UN envoy of climate change Gro Harlem Brundtland said, "The library of life is burning, and we do not even know the titles of the books."

"The world burns" is a strong and urgent metaphor. We see it

Gro Harlem Brundtland delivers a speech during the Equator Prize ceremony at the COP21 Conference in Paris on December 7, 2015. The Equator Prize is awarded to community projects that use conservation and biodiversity to reduce poverty.

again in Thunberg's version where it is our house that is on fire. For Brundtland, it was the entire world, and she likened it to a library containing unknown books and potential knowledge. It is a metaphor that I have used myself—in 2015 I wrote a speech for the then Danish minister for the environment, Kirsten Brosbøl, using the metaphor as an attributed quote and a frame for the arguments about the value of biodiversity and the potential of medical discoveries being lost. We could elaborate on the metaphor and draw on Brundtland's authority:

> Gro Harlem Brundtland once said about the loss of biodiversity, that "The library of life is burning, and we do not even know the titles of all the books." Conservation and valuation of biodiversity is of utmost importance to us all.

We do not know what lifegiving ingredients and business opportunities lie hidden in the burning library section—and we will never know, if we let it burn to the ground.

So, let us stop the fire—together. We need to access the books—together. And we need to share what we find inside—with each other.

## STORY

A story can be defined in many ways. At its most basic, a story has a protagonist living their life in a status quo when something happens and they have to take action to avoid a crisis. There is a climax, and afterward the stakes wind down. Finally, a resolution is found, and a new status quo is established. Stories are good—but preferably, you only chose ONE story that enforces your message.

As a TEDx speaker coach, I have coached numerous TEDx talks. It is always fascinating to meet idealists who want to help humanity by communicating a message through storytelling. Their stories are often intriguing, and so is that of TED itself. Architect Richard Saul Wurman founded the organization in 1984, hoping to gather the most inspiring ideas within technology, entertainment, and design (TED). In 2001 entrepreneur Chris Anderson bought TED. He expanded on the topics and coined the slogan Ideas Worth Spreading. In 2006 TED made all presentations on its website free. Then it exploded in popularity.

The first six TED talks were put online in 2006, and three months later, they had been viewed more than a million times, three years later it was one hundred million times, and in 2012 they reached one billion. According to TED's own website, an average of seventeen talks are viewed every second. This is clearly not just a success of technology—it is a success of concept. What the concept preaches is ONE speaker describing ONE world-changing idea with ONE personal story in a mere eighteen minutes. The key lesson of TED is to limit yourself in duration and stay true to ONE message with ONE personal story. To make your story even more effective, as discussed back in chapter 5, tell your audience how you were convinced of the message in your speech.

## PROP

A prop is an item that you bring along for your speech to use as a symbol of the message. It can be an ice cube, a hat, or some other kind of object. The important thing is that it connects to your message and provides a sensory way to remember your talk. One of the most iconic TED talks was by Microsoft founder Bill Gates on malaria in 2009. Those eighteen minutes have been viewed more than five million times. And most will likely remember that talk for what he brought with him. On a table sat a transparent plastic container, and after talking about the dangers of malaria inflicted by the malaria mosquito, he opened the container and let out a swam of mosquitoes. That sound of the mosquitoes' wings and the feeling of danger is what you will remember, even though you are viewing the talk across time and space, and from a digital screen.

As a speechwriter, I was inspired by that use of a prop, so when I wrote a speech for the then Danish minister for climate, energy and utilities, Rasmus Helveg Petersen, for the World Meteorological Congress in Paris in 2014, I wanted something similar. When it comes to the connection between climate and weather, global averages are the archnemesis of meaning. We wanted to make it concrete and tangible. Something the audience could feel. "The ice is melting at the poles" was not quite enough.

The speech was set to last fifteen minutes, and the event organizers told us that every audience member would have a glass of water for the session. We used the glass in front of each as a prop by arguing they might be able to empty the glass of water during the speech. It might even be healthy. They might even be able to drink three such glasses. But they would not be able to continue doing that for very long without it having consequences. Yet that is what we are doing to the world with global warming. The climate crisis is simply neither sustainable nor healthy.

As a result of his TED talk, I associate the sound of a mosquito with Bill Gates and malaria. As a result of Petersen's speech, I associate a certain type of water glass with the shrinking Arctic ice sheet. By using a prop, you get to decide when—or if—your audience will associate with you and your message. Choose wisely.

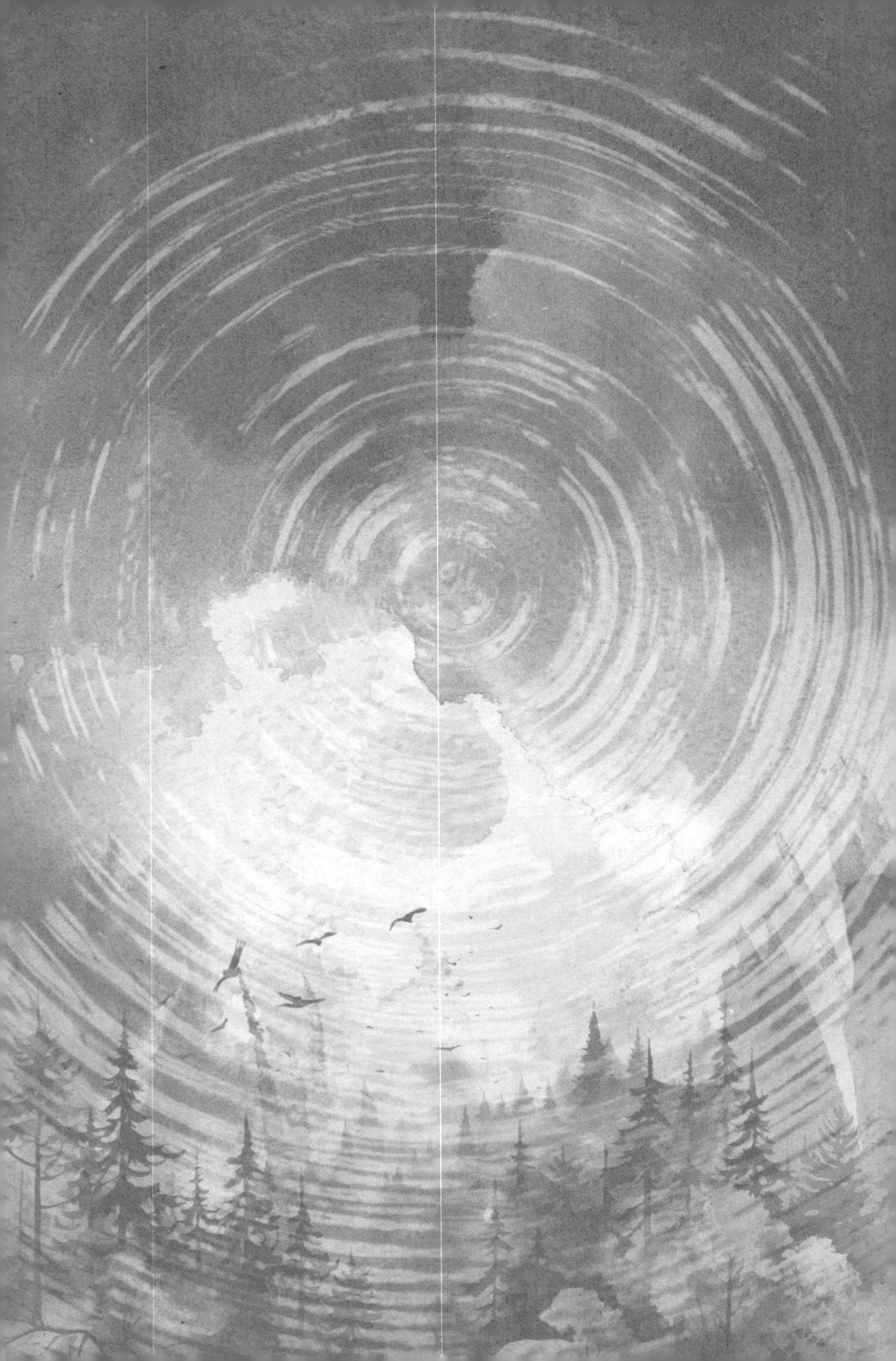

# CHAPTER 8
# THE SOUND OF A LEADER

Simon Lancaster is one of the world's top speechwriters. He started writing speeches for members of Tony Blair's cabinet in the late 1990s, and he now writes speeches for the CEOs of some of the largest companies in the world. Lancaster has taken the old rhetoric tools and combined them with modern neuroscience on how the brain works. He has created a guide to effective communication strategies in his book *Winning Minds: Secrets from the Language of Leadership*.

According to Lancaster, it all comes down to knowing the brain so you are able to speak to it appropriately. The first lesson is that the brain has three parts: instinct, emotion, and logic. Those are the neuroscientific terms for what Aristotle called ethos, pathos, and logos. It's important to understand all three, but instincts are the most important, then emotion, and last comes logic. That is vastly different from how most climate speeches are structured. Instead, they tend to bet it all on the persuasive power of numbers, jargon, and graphs.

## THE INSTINCTIVE BRAIN

The instinctive brain is the place of intuition and the subconscious. It is the part of the brain we share with reptiles. It is the oldest and most used part of the brain. It ensures our survival without us needing to think and controls our bodily functions (such as breathing). Through instinct, our brain might make us lash out or run away if we are scared. The instinctive brain divides everything into *avoid danger* and *claim benefits*. That is why any speaker needs to decide if they want to be perceived as a friend promising benefits or an enemy posing as danger. The audience will decide if a speaker is a friend or an enemy immediately, thus determining if they are worth listening to or if it will be better to run away. The key is that the emotion you are expressing will be the emotion received by the audience.

If you sound hectic with short sentences and superficial breathing, you will create a sense of anxiety in the audience. Attempting to avoid danger, they will have to decide if you are running from a common enemy or if you are the enemy. Longer sentences and deep breaths allow the audience to calm down, feel safe, and be able to listen. They will be more likely to believe you and believe that you know what you are talking about. All of that, simply from the length of your sentences and the depth of your breathing.

Smiling can help you seem welcoming and compassionate to the audience. They are more likely to feel at ease and trust what you say. The instinct for empathy is even stronger when you use the word "we." Simon Lancaster talks about a simple change in making sure that the word "we" features in as many places as possible in a speech. Using "we" and smiling can make people feel seen and recognized. Yet, remember that smiling and saying "we" can also make people think that you do not understand the severity of the climate crisis and that you are delegating responsibility to individuals for a systemic malfunction. It all comes down to who your audience is and making sure to notice their signals of facial expressions and body language.

Another way to speak to people's instincts is through metaphor. Metaphors are a shortcut to the meaning you want to convey—so make sure that it goes where you want it. When using metaphors to invoke instincts, use the most basic ones about food, motion, love, safety, war, and competition. They awaken our emotions and control what we think about a given subject, regardless of if it is organ donation, military engagements, health, or climate action.

This brings us back to Alexander the Great. On the bank of the Indus River, he spoke with empathy and welcome. He did not beat around the bush but got straight to the point in—what I imagine were—calm, long sentences that stressed "we" and "together." He said:

> I observe, gentlemen, that when I would lead you on a new venture you no longer follow me with your old spirit. I have asked you to meet me that we may come to a decision together: are we, upon my advice, to go forward, or, upon yours, to turn back?
>
> Are you afraid that a few natives who may still be left will offer opposition? Come, come! These natives either surrender without a blow or are caught on the run—or leave their country undefended for your taking and when we take it, we make a present of it to those who have joined us of their own free will and fight at our side.
>
> I could not have blamed you for being the first to lose heart if I, your commander, had not shared in your exhausting marches and your perilous campaigns; it would have been natural enough if you had done all the work merely for others to reap the reward. But it is not so. You and I, gentlemen, have shared the labor and shared the danger, and the rewards are for us all. The conquered territory belongs to you.

He seemed open to follow their decision (which he eventually was forced to do). He maintained the "we" regardless of the

This print of Alexander the Great depicts him on a horse speaking to his soldiers.

outcome. Knowing that he was arguing for danger, he tried to make the decision about benefits by promising riches and by downplaying the fight and potential loss to make them feel safe. Alexander uses the metaphor of "labor" for the battle. It gives him at least three advantages.

1. The key advantage is that labor might have dangers and rewards, but labor does not kill you as a military campaign of conquest might. The difference is one of meeting dangers versus death.
2. Another advantage is that labor is continual—as Alexander wants his military campaign to be—whereas a battle is understood to be a definite span of time.

SPEAKING ON CLIMATE

When arguing to prolong the military campaign, Alexander uses a metaphor that would be useful indefinitely.
3. Battle is a high risk and high reward activity, and you need total commitment. Yet labor is something we do regardless of what we believe. By using the labor metaphor for battle, Alexander is arguing that they do not need total commitment.

Alexander's use of a labor metaphor for battle provides him with a way to downplay the risk of death, the short—yet intense—time span of a battle, and the need for total commitment. Yet the labor metaphor also has a downside. Unlike battle and war, labor is something we can decide to stop doing. And that is ultimately what the soldiers did.

## THE EMOTIONAL BRAIN

The emotional part of the brain works largely through hormones. The brain and body have involuntary systems that help regulate our hormones without us needing to do anything. When the body releases hormones, it often has a direct link to our feelings and emotions. For example, if you hug someone long enough, the brain releases a hormone called *oxytocin*, which helps a person feel loved, cared for, or protected—a happy or comforting feeling. When the brain releases *serotonin*, we may feel a sense of pride and self-confidence. *Cortisol* is released when the body is under stress. This hormone helps the body cope but can also induce feelings of stress or anxiety. The more of a given hormone that the brain releases, the stronger the corresponding emotion. Brain science is still a field with a lot of unanswered questions, but it seems that a good story has characters you can identify with, produces oxytocin, contains conflict and dilemmas that produce cortisol, and has a resolution that produces *dopamine*. Dopamine is a chemical messenger in the brain that is released in response to positive experiences and rewards, helping to create feelings of satisfaction and pleasure. In the context of a story, dopamine is released when a story has a satisfying resolution, reinforcing a sense of achievement and joy.

This means repetition is an effective tool for conveying and raising emotions within your audience. Repetition shows that the message is important to you and that emotion is transferred to your audience. They interpret your repetition to reflect your emotions, and they identify with that. The same goes for exaggeration, which can serve to communicate how convinced and passionate you are about your message. In climate communication, repetition and exaggeration are good tools to use with people who already agree with you, but they can be counterproductive when you wish to persuade people who hold an opposing view.

The best way to address the emotions of your audience, however, is through stories. Storytelling creates connectivity and community through identity. When you tell a story, you are asking people to step into a world of your making to experience and feel what your characters are feeling. Through that identification, you can make them see and feel the world from your perspective. This effect is even stronger when you are the protagonist of your story. Another benefit of using storytelling is that humans are tuned into it as a medium. If your audience has been distracted, telling a story will refocus their attention. That is why many public speakers recommend telling stories at regular intervals in your speech. Personally, I would recommend telling one primary story as the backbone of your speech and keeping the speech no longer than twenty minutes.

Alexander the Great also addressed the emotional part of his soldier's brains. He exaggerated their power and thus their likelihood of winning the battle. He repeated the same message—one of confidence in the style of "we can do it"—in different versions to demonstrate his passion and conviction. In that way, he created identity and imposed self-confidence. In the story he told, they were invincible and on the brink of riches. He even ended his speech explicitly recognizing the emotions of the soldiers:

> I could not have blamed you for being the first to lose heart if I, your commander, had not shared in your exhausting marches and your perilous campaigns; it would have been natural enough if you had done all the work merely for others to reap the reward. But it is not so. You and I, gentlemen, have shared the labor and shared the danger, and the rewards are for us all. The conquered territory belongs to you; from your ranks the governors of it are chosen; already the greater part of its treasure passes into your hands, and when all Asia is overrun, then indeed I will go further than the mere satisfaction of our ambitions: the utmost hopes of riches or power which each one of you cherishes will be far surpassed, and whoever wishes to return home will be allowed to go, either with me or without me. I will make those who stay the envy of those who return.

This section is full of emotion: blame, loss of heart, exhaustion, peril, satisfaction, hopes, power, and envy. Alexander's argument rests not on numbers and likelihoods but on feelings and emotions.

## THE LOGICAL BRAIN

The logical brain does not operate on pure logic. It is merely looking to decide if something appears to be logical. To make that decision, it has developed a few shortcuts to save time and energy. These shortcuts are tools you can use to make your argument seem logical—or at least as something you may consider—to avoid it seeming illogical.

It goes something like this: If a speaker has spoken the truth before, that speaker is likely speaking the truth again. If something sounds about right, it most likely is right. If something sounds as though it has been thought through, the brain assumes that it has been.

- One shortcut is that if there are three good reasons to do something, our brain believes it is the right thing to do. This is called the rule of three, and we should divide our arguments into threes—not four or two but three.

- Another shortcut has to do with rhymes. Our brain assumes that if it rhymes, it must be thought through and correct. Rhyming is also helpful in remembering. Use alliteration, rhyme, and other poetic tools.

- A third shortcut is contrast. Contrasting two points demonstrates to the audience that you have weighed the pros and cons, so the brain assumes that it is a solid recommendation. It will appear more logical because you have offered two opposing scenarios.

Alexander the Great used no rational arguments in his speech, but he appealed to the logical part of the brain in several ways. He used the trick of making a long list of victorious battles, thus implying that the next battle would be a victory too. It seemed logical, had it not been for the Persian arrows and war elephants. He even started the speech with a contrast in the shape of a question: Continue or return? This contrast is then expanded upon to include that they could continue to loot what they want from the fleeing Persians or return home and risk it all when the countries rebel against them. He not only made a contrast but also did his best to make his choice appear to be the most beneficial.

There are several rules of three in the speech that run through his central argument. Alexander and his army "have shared the labor and shared the danger, and the rewards are for us all" (labor, danger, reward). The three aim to make the audience think that laboring through danger will lead to rewards. The enemy will "either surrender without a blow or are caught on the run—or leave their country undefended for your taking" (surrender, run, leave undefended).

Again, the rule of three makes the brain assume logic even if the three points are the same thing. If these three are indeed the only options available, then moving forward would be risk-free. The argument is that the war would likely be without battles and without death and loss.

Alexander then appeals to greed and the economic rationality by saying that "the conquered territory belongs to you; from your ranks the governors of it are chosen; already the greater part of its treasure passes into your hands." He is turning greed into economic logic by using the rule of three to create a timeline of labor, danger, and reward, and by recognizing no risk from the Persians, while another rule of three claims that estates, titles, and treasure will be theirs.

In my experience, it is best to speak to the instinctive part of the brain first and most. Then appeal to the emotional brain and last the logical brain. Unless you can combine them. One way to combine the three is to pause when speaking. A pause affects how your audience perceives the length of your sentences and the depth of your breathing. You will seem more friendly, calm, and collected. A pause affects the emotional brain by allowing the stories to create a deeper sense of identification. And a pause will command authority and control allowing you to appeal to logic. Although we know what Alexander the Great said thousands of years ago, we do not know when he paused, only that he paused at the end.

Take a break, let the audience gather their thoughts and consider what you might say next or think about what you just said. Your silence speaks too—give it room. A pause strengthens the impact of what you say before and after. A pause makes the audience more attentive.

A pause seems much longer from the podium or stage than from the floor. We get impatient and think that everybody must be wondering why. But to the audience, it is a delightful break in an often-constant stream of words. We need variation in volume, rhythm, tone and, also, whether we speak or remain silent.

Barack Obama burst into song when he gave a memorial speech on June 26, 2015, in a church in Charleston, South Carolina. He sang "Amazing Grace," and many reporters noted

Barack Obama (*center*) sang as he delivered the eulogy for South Carolina state senator the Reverend Clementa Pinckney.

how impactful this moment was for his presidency. But just before, he was silent for a full thirteen seconds!

He had wondered whether he should sing or not, and he had been working on the speech past midnight the night before. He had doubts walking onto the podium. But he used the thirteen seconds to sharpen the attention of the audience, to heighten their expectations—and to decide what key to sing in.

Thirteen seconds is a long time to be silent with everybody's eyes on you. Try timing it. It feels much longer. And less will do. Five seconds is a fine pause, and it is enough to get back to the thread of your argument and refocus on your message.

Pausing can give you control and authority as a presenter. It shows that you care and that your message is important. And it can increase its meaning to the audience.

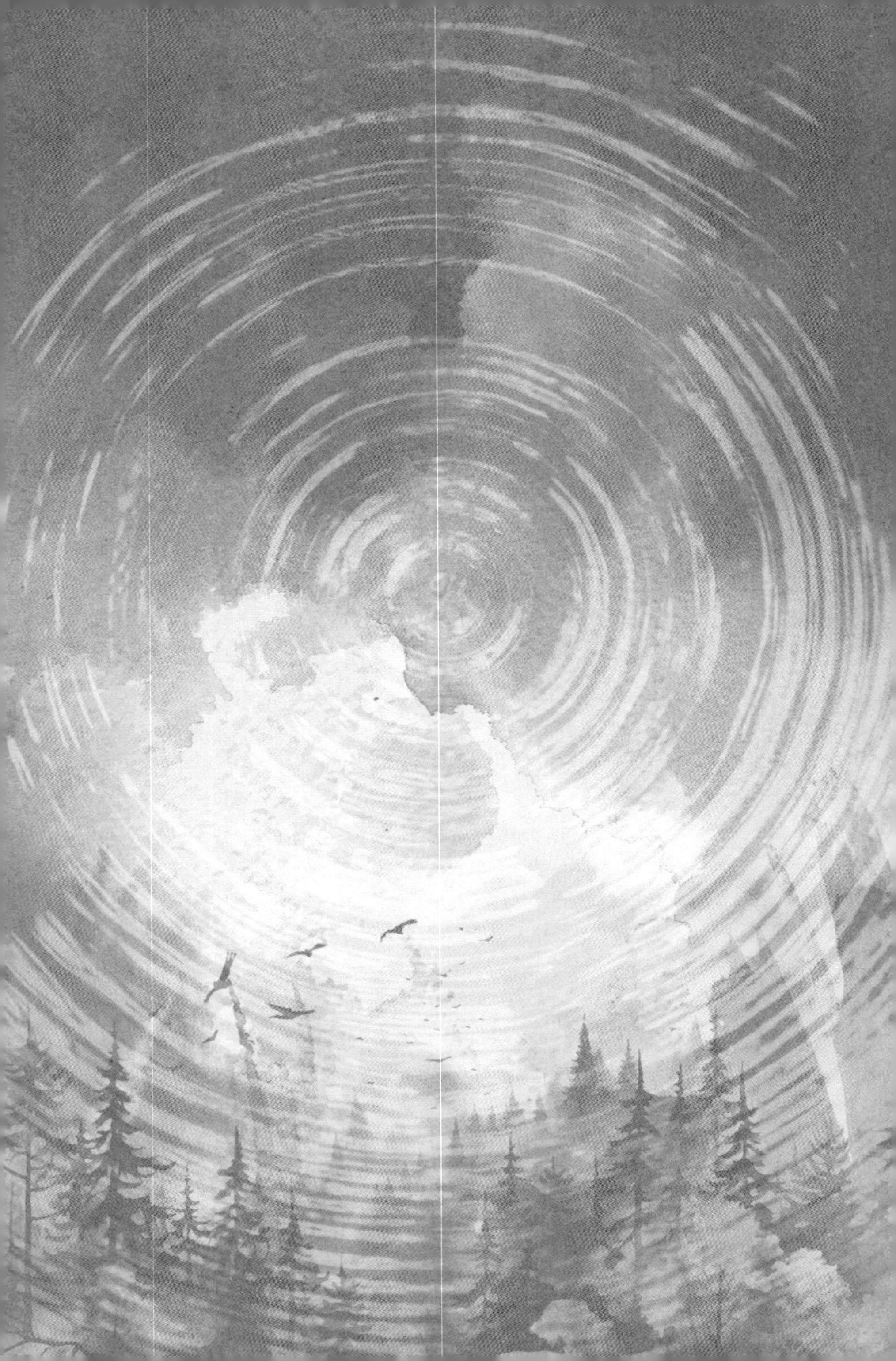

# CHAPTER 9
# MAKE YOUR MESSAGE TRAVEL

Whenever you give a speech, you have two audiences: the people present and listening, and the people the first audience will share your message with afterward. In their 1969 book, *The New Rhetoric: A Treatise on Argumentation*, Chaïm Perelman and Lucie Olbrechts-Tyteca call these two audiences "the particular" (those in front of you) and "the universal" (those who receive your message from other channels). This division highlights the dilemma a speechwriter faces when crafting a message: Should you focus on connecting with the particular audience in front of you at risk of being misunderstood by the universal audience that will see it afterward, or should you try to make your message universal and thus possibly alienate the particular audience? This is a dilemma that I have described in the case of John Winthrop's "city upon a hill," Winston Churchill's war speeches, and Martin Luther King Jr.'s "I Have a Dream."

*The New Rhetoric* argues that if you stay true to your worldview, stand by your emotions, and tell your story the way you see it, then the composition of your audience matters less, and your message can travel safely. By being aware that your message will travel across multiple audiences and media at different times, you can help to control how it is received.

The technological advancements that have occurred since *The New Rhetoric*'s publication have intensified this dilemma. Speeches face challenges today that are different from previous times. In the past, you gave a speech to the people present, and later, if you were lucky, somebody wrote it down or you did so yourself. But with new digital media, words travel farther and wider. That is good, but it also means that you must ensure that the message is correct as it travels through the distracting landscape of digital media and instant gratification.

Franklin D. Roosevelt used the radio to reach the audiences in the living rooms and calm them down during the Great Depression and World War II. His format fit his aim. Obama and Trump, on the other hand, spoke at huge rallies to create enthusiasm for their presidential campaigns. Neither of these could have worked as a fireside chat on the radio. If you have the option, make sure that your format fits your message—and if the format is set, make sure the message fits.

Franklin D. Roosevelt's fireside chats were broadcast across all national radio networks at the time and were intended to be conversations rather than speeches.

Sometimes we get to decide the format or the occasion of the speech. But often we only have to decide what to do with the invitation that is given to us. So the question becomes how to handle it. How do we build our own speech infrastructure to maximize the effect of our message? And what options do the digital technologies provide that were not there before?

## DIGITAL SPEECH INFRASTRUCTURE

When giving a speech, you are performing an art form that is thousands of years old. But you are giving it in modern times, and you decide if that is a barrier or an accelerator for your message. In short, will the smartphones in the pockets of your audience be a potential distraction from your message or powerful technology making your message go further and reach more people?

In the time of Roosevelt, the radio was new technology, and he used it to his advantage. Many claim that John F. Kennedy won against Richard Nixon because he looked better on TV during debates. Bush was the first to use a *live* webcast of the State of the Union. And Barack Obama was the first to fully explore the potential of social media. It was a central piece of his campaign, and he brought that focus with him into the White House. By integrating social media with the traditional State of the Union speech, Obama's chief digital officer, Jason Goldman, demonstrated some of the opportunities that we have available. In 2016, for Obama's last State of the Union speech, the White House created a story about the speech by going behind the curtain and having Obama talk about his expectations and reflections. On official social media accounts, they shared State of the Union quotes from former presidents and pop-cultural references, and they answered questions. They urged people to watch the speech. They even encouraged people to invite others and make a day of it.

## LEADING UP TO THE SPEECH

- **Find a common hashtag.** To tap into the work that event organizers do, ask if there is a shared hashtag for the event or a digital group channel such as #ClimateActionSummit from the UN event of the same name. If they do not have one, you can create one yourself. If you start early, you might be able to shape the popularity of the event and solicit input for the speech you want to give.

- **Create a story around the speech.** Start telling the story about your speech. Announce that you are speaking, share your thoughts about the topic, and discuss the research that went into your speech. Combine the official hashtags with more topic-centric ones to spread your message more widely.

- **Prepare to share.** When the day of the speech approaches and you know what you want to say, prepare to share your message. There is no reason that everybody should not be able to listen to you or read what you had to say on your choice of social platforms.

## DURING THE SPEECH

- **Arrange for pics, or it didn't happen.** When thinking about the afterlife of your speech, do not underestimate the power of a picture or a short recording. You might not be able to make one yourself, so get a friend to do it for you. The important thing is to get the audience's reaction as well. That will increase the sense of community when people are watching it alone. That is the case with TED talks where you see both the speaker and the audience. You might be watching them on your phone all alone, but you will feel part of something greater across time and space.

- **Consider your background.** When your audience is watching you, they are also watching whatever is behind you. And when they take pictures or record a video of you, they also capture what is behind you. What is behind you can serve as a distraction or an amplifier of your message. Why have a boring background when it can include your choice of hashtag, your message in slogan form, or a picture highlighting your message?

- **Ask the audience to share.** Some people will naturally share your message with friends on social media or in conversation. Others will not. If you want your message to travel as far as possible, make sure that you ask the audience to share. You can give them the time to write your message as a social media post, encourage them to ask questions online afterward, or pose a question and ask them to answer on social media. For example, consider asking them to talk about their emotional response to the climate crisis, the values they hold dear in solutions, or what term they think is best for describing the crisis. It can even be which lessons from history they think we can learn from.

Behind any speech is a stack of research on the topic that did not make the final cut. If it reinforces your message, use it. During Obama's State of the Union speech, the White House staff was live-posting content with additional quotes, pictures, memes, and infographics that elaborated on the arguments and messages in the speech. They allowed people to take a deep dive into those sections that they felt most strongly about. Every time a photographer snapped a photo, it did not take long for Obama's team to share that photo along with video clips of audience reactions. They even spurred on interaction by asking activists and opinion leaders to participate in the debate in the comments and share their experiences.

## AFTER THE SPEECH IS GIVEN

- **Monitor the speech's key words.** Your speech does not end when you leave the podium or the stage. The final punctuation does not mark the finish. If you have done well, your speech will engage a lot of people. They will have questions, comments, and reactions to share. And you will be able to help them by participating in the debate both in person and online. Be sure to engage with the people who respond to social media posts about your speech with their own comments and questions—including those who disagree with you. Even negative reactions carry your message further, and most people will be pleasantly surprised that you took the time to respond.

- **Transform your speech to other formats.** When the speech is over, look at the content you gathered and polished. Look through the research you did and share links for people to dive deeper. Transform your speech script into an op-ed or a blog post. Share pictures of your speech on your platforms with your recollection of the event. If you have a video recording, edit it to fit social media and share it again.

- **Continue the story about the speech.** What was it like to deliver your speech? That is a question people will be interested in, and you should tell that story too. It will be relevant for the audience of the speech and for the people who participated online. But it will also be a way for you to start a conversation about your message—the story about the speech.

## SPEECHES ONLINE

Some speeches are in front of an in-person audience. Others are fully digital and given online as a webinar, video presentation, or similar. In either case, your speech will be most powerful if there is an indication of an actual audience. So if you give a speech online, get inspiration from TED talks rather than Zoom meetings. You want to create a sense of community across the many different screens.

In my experience, in an online presentation you have neither the interaction between audience and speaker nor the group dynamic inside the audience. That is because from the individual screen, you can't sense the collective sentiment of the audience in a group. It's hard to hear and see if people are moved, empowered, or put off by a speech. To compensate for the loss of the physical room, create a connection to someone you cannot see—someone who is listening to you at a different time. The screen tends to remove personality and emotion. You must fight a little harder to keep that in and refrain from simply presenting the numbers. Make it a little more human and be a little more open about mistakes, fiascoes, and feelings. Doing this will help bridge the gap increased by the screen.

The screen can also distract people because your facial expressions and body language cannot keep them involved in the same way. Make sure to tell people what to expect, how far along you are, and what the key messages are. This can be as simple as mentioning how long you will likely talk, presenting a short program at the start of your speech, and returning to each point when moving on. You can do this verbally or by using text or visuals in a slideshow.

If you are new to digital presentations, remember that people likely will be watching you in close-up. Be mindful of your appearance so that it does not distract from your message. Choose a light source that does not make you look scary, and put the camera above eye level to avoid anyone focusing on your nostrils. Check the sound quality beforehand, and do not talk too closely to the microphone. Those are the basics.

Here, too, you can steal some tricks from TED talks. TED talks use the audience as an assumed presence to create a herd mentality beyond the screen. The presence of the audience is often only implied by the sound of applause, the direction of the camera, or the silhouettes of the front row audience. You can do the same with a few friends. Also notice that TED talks are set on a stage, giving authority. And they use only very simple visual slides in the background—no text to read that might distract the audience from the verbal speech. The focus should always be on the speaker and not the slides. And last, TED talks are heavy on the side of personal stories to bridge the gap created by the screen.

Essentially, it is a very simple and strict concept: choose an interesting speaker to present one unique idea wrapped in a personal story in front of a small and dedicated audience, and record it on video to share online. It works. It spreads ideas worth sharing and starts conversations on social platforms, in living rooms, across dinner tables, and in cantinas and cafés all over. And those conversations are where the magic happens—where change starts. You can spur those conversations along, and you can even take your message directly into those conversations.

TED talks are presented on a stage with the speaker often standing on a red carpet looking out at an audience with a screen behind them. Here Rune Hjarnø Rasmussen talks about kinship and biodiversity at TEDxTralee in Ireland.

## A CONVERSATION GUIDE FOR BREAKING CLIMATE SILENCE

Two-thirds of all young people are worried about the climate crisis, yet only one-third has regular climate conversations. The phenomenon is called *climate silence*. As we worry yet rarely talk about climate and the solutions have been individualized and removed from collective action, we feel alone with the fate of the world on our shoulders. That leads to climate anxiety and inaction. Giving a speech on climate is an ideal opportunity to break climate silence and demonstrate to others that none of us are alone.

The reasons we do not speak about climate are diverse. It is considered a downer that will wreck the good vibes (so were slavery, civil rights, women's right to vote, and labor organizing). People are afraid of being called hypocrites because they do not live according to their beliefs. When we collectivize climate action through speeches as in political or systemic solutions, it will no longer be an individual responsibility, and we will no longer be accused of being hypocrites. And climate is a polarized topic with an "us versus them" mentality, where different sides yell at each other without the issue ever really being addressed. What do we do?

The British organization Climate Outreach has worked on creating climate conversations for more than twenty years. They argue that conversations have immense impact and can shift opinions and values when they're built on trust and common ground. That is why we should ask open questions and find

Youth are getting more opportunities to speak out about climate. In 2021 Greta Thunberg attended the Youth4Climate: Driving Ambition conference in Milan, Italy. This conference was held prior to COP26 to give young climate leaders a chance to share proposals to address the climate crisis.

emotional common ground by listening and staying curious. We might find that all people have issues they care about that are affected by the climate crisis. We just need to make the connection. More than speeches, conversations have the potential to reach beyond the like-minded crowd and engage those who still need persuading.

Your speech is an excellent opportunity to do that. Good speeches lead to conversations. If audiences are persuaded to change, they will be asked to defend and explain themselves in their networks, around the dinner table, or in the cafeteria. Here is what to remember if you want to make your message stick in climate conversations:

- **Speeches are about *your* perspective, but climate conversations are about *everyone's* perspectives!** You get to learn about your conversation partner and their perspective on the world. Respect how they see the world and what they prioritize and value. The people you want to reach are likely used to being judged and blamed in climate conversations, making them defensive and withdrawn. You should try to open the doors and make them feel heard.

- **Climate is about values and emotions, so listen closely and ask curious questions.** What are their values, and how do they feel about the state of the world? Explore their emotions, values, and worldview. Don't insist on talking about the climate crisis—talk about what matters to them and connect it to climate. Help them see how climate action is a natural consequence of their emotions, values, and worldview.

- **Share your own story and what made you change tracks.** Your arguments are likely to resonate better than abstract numbers and statistics. Your story is yours and cannot be contested like statistics, source material, and motives. Being human, you are relatable, and hearing your earnest story will help more than any IPCC report. Maybe it will inspire them to tell their story.

- **Remain calm and stay connected—change can happen slowly.** A conversation might not lead to visible change, but you are sowing seeds that will grow when people are ready, and you might not get to see it. Breaking the climate silence is a goal in itself. Staying connected will mean that you can help this along, but you need to stay calm, or you risk reinforcing the very divisions you are trying to break down.

- **Invite them to take action together or as part of a wider community of action.** Most people believe that you have to be convinced about a problem to take action, but it goes the other way too. When you work with others, you will persuade yourself that it is needed. And if you are worried about the future, taking action in a community is the best way to feel better. It helps the feeling of inaction, and it helps to not be alone. You may still struggle with the right actions, but we all do, so start by acknowledging that it is hard.

The psychology behind climate silence is interesting. As humans, we generally feel uncomfortable when our actions do not fit with our opinions. To handle this paradox (cognitive dissonance) we have three routes to take. We can change our opinions, we can ignore or explain away the gap, or we can change our actions.

The premise of this book is that you care deeply about the

climate crisis and that so do most people when they connect their values to the impacts of the climate crisis. That means that pro-climate opinions already exist, and we do not want them to change. We want the actions to change to fit said opinions, and to do that we have to break climate silence and thus move beyond ignoring the gap or explaining it away. No more excuses—we have to open our minds to solutions and actions we can all take. The promise is that this will feel much better for most people.

These actions will not be easy. There will be setbacks. Change is never easy, and some people will be asked to break from their network and sense of identity. That is no small ask. As humans we draw on different motivations. We reflect on what is the right thing to do, what we gain from it, and what would be pleasant for us. But we also choose what is easy, what our habits are, and what we think others do. Have these in mind when proposing solutions that will bridge the gap between pro-climate opinion and action.

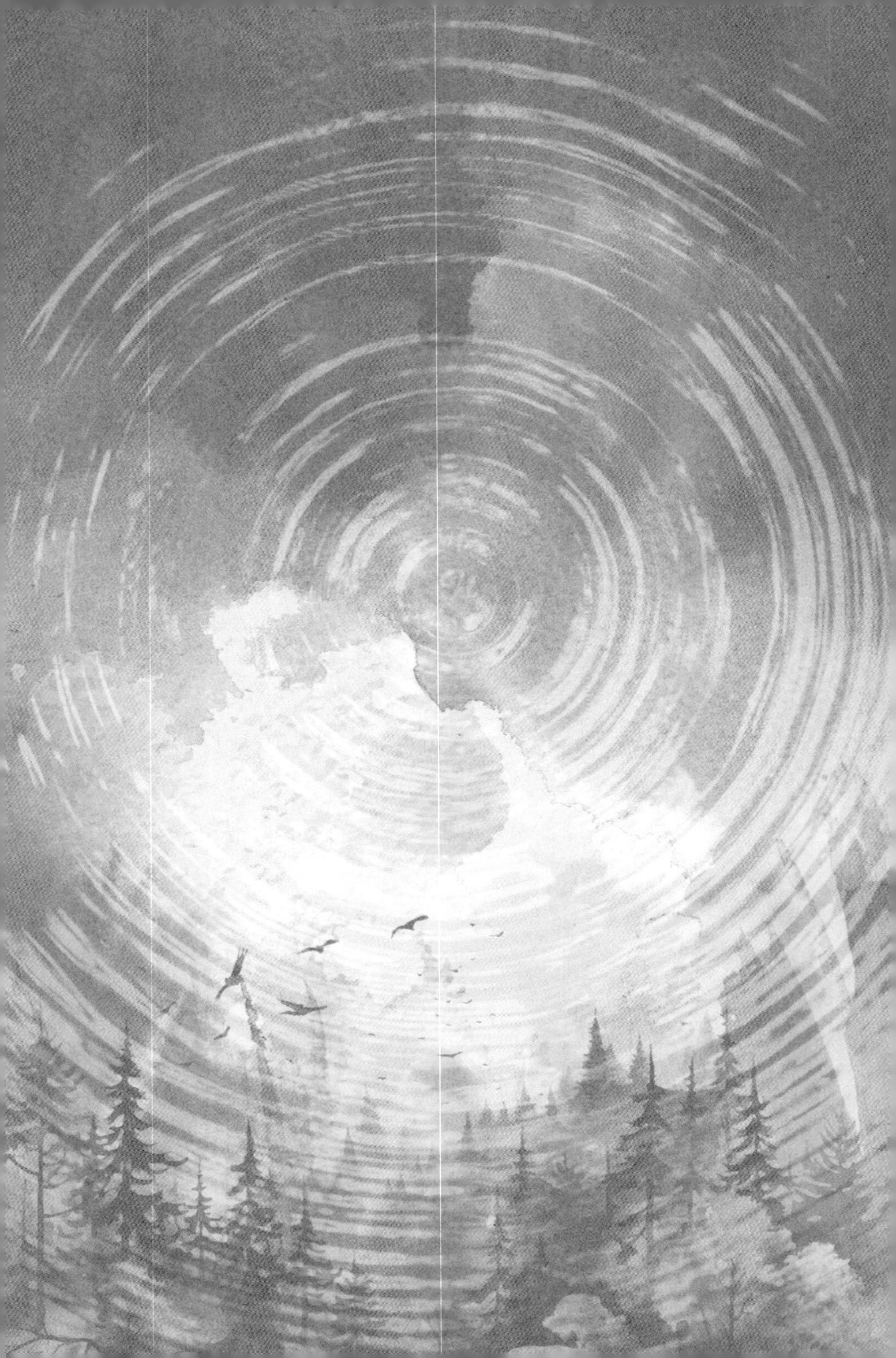

# AFTERWORD

*You can do it—we can do it.* And you will get better. Hopefully, this book will help. And it might help knowing that people have done it before. All good speakers have practiced and gotten better. So will you. This is only the beginning.

We can solve the climate crisis. Science has long understood the challenge we face. We have so many solutions, and studies show that many are cheaper than the alternatives. We are many who are pushing for action, and our numbers are growing by the day. We have created change before, and we can do it again.

And not just small-scale change. Massive social change such as the abolitionist movement freeing enslaved people across the world, the suffragette movement leading the battle for women's right to vote, the environmental and climate movement protecting our planet and the natural world—they all started with a dedicated group of citizens.

*YOU can make a difference.* We can do it because we have done it before.

*Sharing is caring.* I wrote this book to make it easier for you to share your message with the world. And I hope that you will share this book with others to help them do the same. Because you are not alone. You are standing on the shoulders of giants, and what might appear as the peak of darkness might just as well be the moment before dawn.

We are many, and we have a long history.

## AN ECHO THROUGH THE AGES

The end of the last ice age about twelve thousand years ago could not have been anything but a crisis for humans living at the time. It would have affected where they could live, what they could eat, what tools they had available, and how they organized their societies. Unfortunately, we know very little of how they managed that change. Most religions have a myth about giant floods, and some historians believe this common story is a reference to the end of the ice age. Even if we never know that history, there are more recent records of natural disasters that caused massive climate disruptions. One such event was the Fimbul Winter.

This engraving depicts Ragnarok with gods fighting against the serpent, Jörmungandr, and the wolf, Fenrir.

## FIMBUL WINTER AND RAGNAROK

Across Scandinavia, in sources such as the *Eddas*, the *Kalevala*, and the *Völuspá*, epic poems that chronicle the history of the area, it is believed that a three-year-long Fimbul Winter came as a prelude for Ragnarok—the end of the world as we know it. The Fimbul Winter was long believed to be a myth, yet recently archaeological records found it to be a historical incident that impacted much of the Northern Hemisphere and that has been enshrined in myth for fifteen hundred years. Now we know that in the year 536, a climate catastrophe struck, caused by a massive volcano erupting in Iceland in the spring and loading the atmosphere with ash and dust particles, effectively blocking sunlight in Scandinavia, the Baltics, and northern Germany for three years. The effect was devastating and felt as far away as China.

People lost daylight, and the sun dimmed as if it were a moon even in the height of summer. At night the stars disappeared, making it hard to navigate. The light of the moon was lost, making it impossible to track time on the calendar. Plants wouldn't grow, and no food led to hunger and starvation. Humans and animals died in large numbers. Temperatures dropped, and the winter came back taking over the summer. Archeologists estimate that Sweden and Norway lost half their population the first winter. But then came another year. And then another. Three years of constant winter with dimmed sun, no stars, and no moon. Some places were left uninhabited for a hundred years. But during this time, gold was abundant in the graves archaeologists have found signaling either the need to please the gods or to hide your treasure.

This historical event made a lasting mark on Nordic culture and mythology. People struggled to interpret the events and pass on what they learned. They came to believe the Fimbul Winter as the outcome of humanity breaking the bond with nature—or, you might say, that growing tension in the human-nature relationship challenged human survival or even that humanity's suicidal war on nature had caused a fading natural world with severe consequences for us as a species.

It was so serious that it was not enough to make it a warning from the gods to humans. It had to be a warning to the gods themselves. And so in Nordic mythology, Odin, king of the gods, humbly asks the seer for knowledge about the future and the end of the world in the *Völuspá*.

In another story, Odin enters a competition of wisdom quizzing giants on the fate of the world. They respond knowingly:

> The first is this, that there shall come that winter which is called the Fimbul Winter: in that time snow shall drive from all quarters; frosts shall be great then, and winds sharp; there shall be no virtue in the sun. Those winters shall proceed three in succession, and no summer between; but first shall come three other winters, such that over all the world there shall be mighty battles. In that time brothers shall slay each other for greed's sake, and none shall spare father or son in manslaughter and in incest; so it says in Völuspá:
>
> > Brothers shall strive | and slaughter each other;
> > Own sisters' children | shall sin together;
> > Ill days among men, | many a whoredom:
> > An axe-age, a sword-age, | shields shall be cloven;
> > A wind-age, a wolf-age, | ere the world totters.
>
> Then shall happen what seems great tidings: the Wolf shall swallow the sun; and this shall seem to men a great harm. Then the other wolf shall seize the moon, and he also shall work great ruin; the stars shall vanish from the heavens.

The Fimbul Winter was a real event that became history. History became legend. Legend became myth, and myth turned into fairy tales told to children. And so, according to historian of religion Rune Hjarnø Rasmussen, the story of the devastating Fimbul Winter and its message about the consequences of the broken bond between humans and nature morphed into a personal story. But it is still there because stories live rent-free in our personal and collective memory.

## HISTORICAL LESSON FROM PERSONAL STORIES

In societies and times without widespread literacy in writing, verbal storytelling is the best way to convey lessons and commit them to collective memory. That, too, testifies to the power of the ancient art of speeches. The best stories carry messages and meaning far and wide through time and space. By using the conventions of fairy tales, a story will be better remembered and more accurately retold. In this case, we might learn from the experiences of people living fifteen hundred years ago.

Imagine how it might look if a story conveyed the lessons of the Fimbul Winter. It would have a character symbolizing humanity and a character symbolizing nature. They would have a close connection that would turn bad. And it would have dire consequences—for both but mostly for the character symbolizing humanity. It might be a tragic story of the human spouse of a nature being abandoning its family and feeling the consequences.

Such a story exists. You might even know it: it is the original story of the Little Mermaid by Danish poet Hans Christian Andersen. Disney adapted the story into a popular animated movie, in which the mermaid marries the prince. Andersen's version of the story, however, ends in tragedy, as the prince marries another human and forgets about the mermaid, leaving her all alone on a cliff dreaming of reconnecting with her love on land.

## AGNETE AND THE MERMAN

But the story is even older. Hans Christian Andersen wrote his story in 1836 and built it on the Danish folklore tale of "Agnete and the Merman." In this story a human woman called Agnete falls in love with a merman, marries him, and starts a family below the waves. They are happy with lots of gold and seven children. One day Agnete wishes to attend church and see her human family again. The merman agrees to this under the condition that she does not look at the statues of the saints in the church. When on land, Agnete breaks her promise and so disavows her family under the sea. Her husband, the merman, enters the church and desperately pleas with her to come home, to reconnect and reforge their relationship.

This is my translation:

> His hair was pure as gold, his eyes were full of tears.
> "Agnete, Agnete! Come to the Sea with me. Your little children long for you."
> "Yes, let them long for me as long as they wish. Them I will never be with again."
> "Oh, but think of the big ones and think of the small, but mostly think about the little one still in the crib."
> "No, I will never think of the big and the small, and least of all on the little one still in the crib."
> The merman raised his right hand: "Twilight and darkness across all land!"
> Then came twilight and dark clouds hiding both land and town.

That is how folklore told the story of humans breaking the bond with nature. In the story, balance is only restored when in

> This bronze sculpture was installed in a canal near the Højbro Bridge in Copenhagen, Denmark. It is based on the story of "Agnete and the Merman" and shows the merman and his seven sons perpetually waiting for Agnete to return.

the darkness, Agnete returns to the sea to a much more meager existence than before. The bond is remade, but trust is lost. This motif is not only in the *Little Mermaid*. It is in many Scandinavian folklore stories—and many Disney movies too.

But let us dive deeper. Stories create identification, and as listeners we are asked to abandon our own reality for a second to see the world through someone else's perspective. We are the humans—and so the merman is asking us to "think of the big ones and think of the small, but mostly think about the little one still in the crib." We get to decide if we take his advice or face "Twilight and darkness across all land!"

What would the children of Agnete and the merman say, if

they spoke out? If we imagine for a moment that we ARE their children, what would we say? What would we tell Agnete who broke the bond?

I don't know about you, but I might sound something like this: "How dare you! We are your own children. Are we even on your list of priorities?"

## WHAT THEN? REFORGING THE BOND

Ragnarok is the end of the world in Norse mythology. Or maybe the end of our world or at least the world as we know it. There is a world after. When Odin quizzed the giants, he also asked about the world after Ragnarok, and they responded that Earth shall emerge from the sea all green and fair. The world shall be plentiful, and it will be peopled once again. The sun shall be reborn. The children of gods and giants shall live. They will meet at the mythical Ida plains, where they will talk and remember their wisdom and speak of what happened before.

The story of Agnete and the Merman ends with the world draped in darkness and Agnete forced back to the sea. That is the Fimbul Winter. But after the three years of Fimbul Winter, the sunlight returned, and the plants grew again. Humans and animals ate and lived and multiplied. Areas lost were repopulated. How do we learn from these experiences, and how do we pass on a better world to those who will call us ancestors?

We might start reforging the bond with nature by acknowledging that humans *are* nature. We are relatives. We are related to—and dependent on—the natural world, we are related to the past, and we are related to the future. We understand our present as the middle of a line between the former present we call the past and the anticipated present we call the future. So, how can we understand the present if the past is forgotten and the future is unknown? By talking about it.

And unlike the Fimbul Winter and the betrayal of Agnete, $CO_2$ emissions are human-made, and humans are capable of stopping the catastrophe. The Fimbul Winter and the fate of Agnete are warnings, not futures set in stone. They speak of humans breaking the bond with nature, but you can speak up about how we remake that bond.

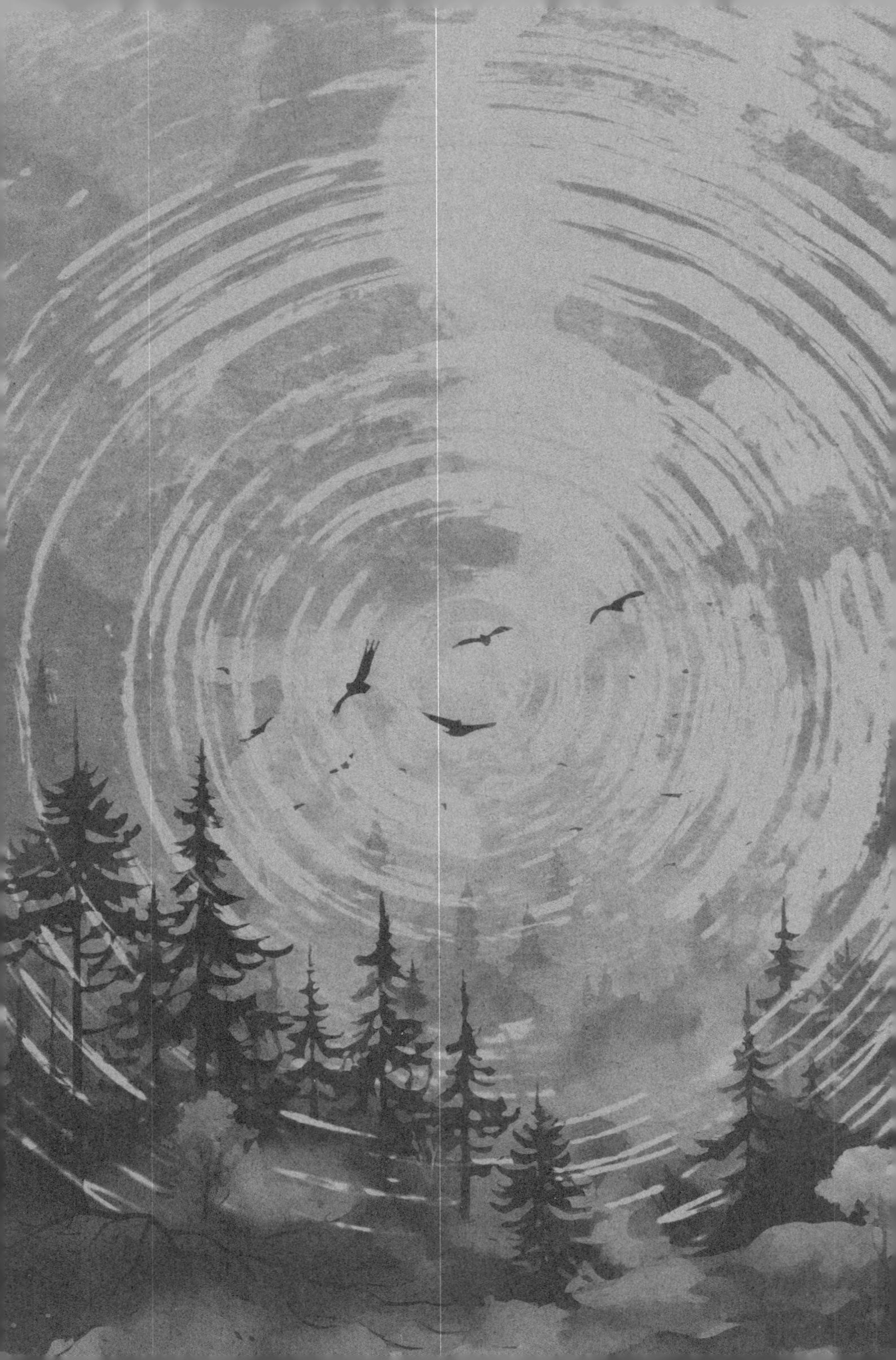

# SOURCE NOTES

8 "By understanding the plight . . . and our own.": David Murray, personal communication with the author, April 2014.

8 "Wow. I've been . . . it is arresting.": Tom Rosshirt, personal communication with the author, April 2014.

11 "Now is the . . . and the playtime.": W. E. B. Du Bois quoted in Lewis Femi, "Biography of W.E.B. Du Bois, Black Activist and Scholar," ThoughtCo, last modified October 18, 2020, https://www.thoughtco.com/w-e-b-du-bois-innovative-activist-45312.

15 "Now strange words . . . of something fresh.": Aristotle, *Rhetoric*, trans. W. Rhys Roberts (New York: Modern Library, 1954), 141, http://classics.mit.edu/Aristotle/rhetoric.html.

17 "This generation has . . . of fossil fuels.": Marianne Lavella, "A 50th Anniversary Few Remember: Warning on Carbon Dioxide," *Jackson Free Press*, February 2, 2015, https://www.jacksonfreepress.com/news/2015/feb/02/50th-anniversary-few-remember-lbjs-warning-carbon-/.

17 "If we want . . . the extra costs.": Milton Friedman and Rose Friedman, *Free to Choose: A Personal Statement* (New York: Harcourt Brace Jovanovich, 1979), 218.

18 "sustainable development": United Nations, *Our Common Future: The World Commission on Environment and Development* (Oxford: Oxford University Press, 1987), vi.

18 "Of all the . . . that subject alone.": Margaret Thatcher, "Speech to the United Nations General Assembly (Global Environment)," November 8, 1989, United Nations Building, New York, Margaret Thatcher Foundation, transcript, https://www.margaretthatcher.org/document/107817.

19 "Coming up here ... left to go.": Severn Cullis-Suzuki, "Speech at U.N. Conference on Environment and Development," Rio de Janeiro, Brazil, 1992, American Rhetoric, transcript, https://www.americanrhetoric.com/speeches/severnsuzukiunearthsummit.htm.

19 "In my anger, ... list of priorities?": Cullis-Suzuki.

21 "Global Marshall Plan": Al Gore, *Earth in the Balance: Ecology and the Human Spirit* (Boston: Houghton Mifflin, 1992), 297–301.

21 "People all over ... let's renew it.": Al Gore quoted in "'An Inconvenient Truth' Wins the Documentary Feature Oscar," YouTube video, 1:42, posted by Oscars, February 4, 2016, https://www.youtube.com/watch?v=3e6LKm1QcXI.

22 "critical thresholds beyond ... and/or irreversibly": Intergovernmental Panel on Climate Change (IPCC), *Climate Change 2021: The Physical Science Basis. Contribution of Working Group I to the Sixth Assessment Report of the Intergovernmental Panel on Climate Change*, ed. V. Masson-Delmotte et al. (Cambridge: Cambridge University Press, 2021), 30.

23 "an existential threat": Joe Biden, "Transcript of Joe Biden's DNC Speech," CNN, August 20, 2020, https://www.cnn.com/2020/08/20/politics/joe-biden-speech-transcript/index.html.

23 "battles of our time": Joe Biden, "Read Joe Biden's Full Victory Speech after Winning the Presidential Election," PBS, November 7, 2020, https://www.pbs.org/newshour/politics/read-joe-bidens-full-victory-speech-after-winning-the-presidential-election.

23 "Climate change will ... of our planet.": Joe Biden, "Roadblocks," December 28, 2020, in Wilmington, DE, rev, transcript, https://www.rev.com/blog/transcripts/joe

-biden-speech-transcript-on-roadblocks-between-his-transition-team-trumps-administration.

23 "A cry for . . . any more clear.": Joe Biden, "Inaugural Address," January 20, 2021, Washington, DC, The White House, transcript, https://www.whitehouse.gov/briefing-room/speeches-remarks/2021/01/20/inaugural-address-by-president-joseph-r-biden-jr/.

23 "Humanity has . . . gates of hell.": António Guterres, "Opening Remarks at the Climate Ambition Summit," United Nations, New York, September 20, 2023, transcript, https://www.un.org/sg/en/content/sg/speeches/2023-09-20/secretary-generals-opening-remarks-the-climate-ambition-summit.

26 "Cogito, ergo sum": René Descartes, *Discourse on the Method*, trans. Donald A. Cress (Indianapolis: Hackett, 1998), 18.

31 "My message is . . . How dare you!": Greta Thunberg, *No One Is Too Small to Make a Difference* (London: Penguin, 2019), 49.

33–35 "Emperor penguins always . . . adapt to it.": Rune Kier Nielsen, unpublished speech, 2013.

36–37 "In Afghanistan lives . . . to appreciate that.": Kirsten Brosbøl, "We Must Appreciate That We Get to Learn," Danish Ministry of Environment, delivered on April 20, 2015, unpublished.

39 "What is happening? . . . you for it!": Merlin quoted in Norris J. Lacy, ed., *Lancelot-Grail: 5 Volumes, the Old French Vulgate & Post-Vulgate Cycles in Translation* (London: Routledge, 1993), 115–135.

41 "We Christians, together . . . to destroy it.": Pope Francis, "Speech to United Nations," New York, *Guardian* (US edition), September 25, 2015, transcript, https://

www.theguardian.com/environment/2015/sep/25/pope-franciss-speech-to-the-un-in-full.

42 "The natural world . . . my own eyes.": David Attenborough and Jonnie Hughes, *A Life on Our Planet: My Witness Statement and a Vision for the Future* (London: Ebury, 2020*)*; *David Attenborough: A Life on Our Planet*, directed by Jonnie Hughes (Netflix, 2020).

42 "You, me, and . . . we damage ourselves.": David Attenborough quoted in Nicole Morley, "'If We Damage the Natural World, We Damage Ourselves'—Sir David Attenborough Urges Humans to Protect the Environment," Wales Online, April 3, 2019, https://www.walesonline.co.uk/news/uk-news/sir-david-attenborough-urges-humans-16065887.

42–43 "Since [the] time . . . survival and development.": Xi Jinping quoted in Huaxia, "Full Text: Remarks by Chinese President Xi Jinping at Leaders Summit on Climate," XinhuaNet, April 22, 2021, http://www.xinhuanet.com/english/2021-04/22/c_139899289.htm.

47 "lost the environmental communications battle": Frank Luntz quoted in Oliver Burkeman, "Memo Exposes Bush's New Green Strategy," *Guardian* (US edition), March 3, 2003, https://www.theguardian.com/environment/2003/mar/04/usnews.climatechange.

47 "'Climate change' is . . . less emotional challenge.": Frank Luntz, "The Environment: A Cleaner, Safer, Healthier America," Luntz Research Companies, accessed September 4, 2024, 142, https://www.sourcewatch.org/images/4/45/LuntzResearch.Memo.pdf.

47–48 "The 'international fairness' . . . to support it.": Luntz, 137.

50 "Our house is . . . Because it is.": Thunberg, *No One*, 25.

51 "think of environmental . . . of the truth.": Luntz, "The Environment," 132.

51 "Adults keep saying . . . you to panic.": Thunberg, *No One*, 24–25.

51 "the first (and . . . sincerity and concern.": Luntz, "The Environment," 132.

51 "We are now . . . bigger your responsibility.": Thunberg, *No One*, 82.

52 "the most important . . . to sound science.": Luntz, "The Environment," 138.

53 "the existential threat . . . by climate change": Joe Biden quoted in "Read the Full Speech: Joe Biden's Remarks to the 2020 Democratic National Convention," NBC News, August 20, 2020, https://www.nbcnews.com/politics/2020-election/read-full-speech-joe-biden-s-remarks-2020-democratic-national-n1237620.

53 "there is no . . . and our world.": "Biden's Climate Plan," Climate Change Resources, accessed August 13, 2024, https://climatechangeresources.org/learn-more/federal-government/executive/bidens-climate-plan/.

53 "I don't even . . . a climate crisis.": Kamala Harris quoted in Emily Atkins, "Damn Right It's a Climate Crisis," *New Republic*, June 27, 2019, https://newrepublic.com/article/154372/damn-right-climate-crisis.

53 "Climate change has . . . become a reality.": Kamala Harris, "Remarks by Vice President Harris on Climate Resilience," The White House, August 1, 2022, https://www.whitehouse.gov/briefing-room/speeches-remarks/2022/08/01/remarks-by-vice-president-harris-on-climate-resilience/.

54 "freedom means that . . . drink clean water.": Barack Obama, "A Full Transcript of Barack Obama's Speech at the 2024 Democratic National Convention," *Time*, August 21, 2024, https://time.com/2024/08/21/full-transcript-barack-obama-2024-dnc-speech/.

55 "the freedom to . . . the climate crisis.": Kamala Harris, "Remarks by Vice President Harris During Keynote Address at the Democratic National Convention," August 22, 2024, Chicago, The White House, https://www.whitehouse.gov/briefing-room/speeches-remarks/2024/08/22/remarks-by-vice-president-harris-during-keynote-address-at-the-democratic-nation-convention/.

55 "Freedom. When Republicans . . . that you love.": Tim Walz quoted in Rebecca Falconer, "Read: Tim Walz's Full Speech at the 2024 DNC," Axios, August 22, 2024, https://www.axios.com/2024/08/22/tim-walz-dnc-speech-full-transcript.

56 "To put it . . . start the healing.": António Guterres, "Secretary-General's Address at Columbia University: 'The State of the Planet,'" United Nations, December 2, 2020, transcript, https://www.un.org/sg/en/content/sg/speeches/2020-12-02/address-columbia-university-the-state-of-the-planet.

56 "a climate catastrophe . . . descent towards chaos.": Guterres.

56 "in a race . . . race to net-zero.": Guterres.

56 "stop the plunder . . . start the healing.": Guterres.

58 "The era of . . . boiling has arrived.": António Guterres, "Secretary-General's Opening Remarks at Press Conference on Climate," United Nations, New York, July 27, 2023, transcript, https://www.un.org/sg/en/content/sg/speeches/2023-07-27/secretary-generals-opening-remarks-press-conference-climate.

61 "the greatest crisis . . . of our species": Bill McKibben, *Falter: Has the Human Game Begun to Play Itself Out?* (New York: Henry Holt, 2019), 43.

61 "the climate crisis . . . have ever faced": Greta Thunberg, *The Climate Book: The Facts and the Solutions* (London: Penguin Books, 2023), 87.

63 "The most insidious . . . women to vote.": Clover Hogan, "Activism Works, Hosted by Debatable," YouTube video, 1:42:27, posted by Kite Insights, June 27, 2023, https://www.youtube.com/watch?v=nfD5gnPV7XM&t=6s.

70 "I also was . . . stand in that.": Marshall Ganz, "Why Stories Matter," *Sojourners*, March 2009, https://sojo.net/magazine/march-2009/why-stories-matter.

71 "The past, present . . . as a story.": Victor W. Turner and Edward M. Bruner, eds., *The Anthropology of Experience* (Champaign: University of Illinois Press), 1986, 141.

73 "the mythical quilombo philosophy": Rune Kier Nielsen, *Race for Agency: Discursive Stories About Race and the Narration of Hope in Salvador, Brazil* (Odense, Denmark. akademia.dk, 2007), 45.

76 "Americans have called . . . of our time.": Joe Biden, "Acceptance Speech," Wilmington, DE, November 7, 2020, *New York Times*, transcript, https://www.nytimes.com/article/biden-speech-transcript.html.

78 "life or death challenges": Al Gore, "Al Gore: The Climate Crisis Is the Battle of Our Time, and We Can Win," *New York Times*, September 20, 2019, https://www.nytimes.com/2019/09/20/opinion/al-gore-climate-change.html.

78 "inflection points": Biden, "Acceptance Speech."

79 "Our house is on fire": Greta Thunberg, Address at World Economic Forum: Our House Is On Fire - Jan 25, 2019," Iowa State University Archives of Women's Political Communication, January 25, 2019, https://awpc.cattcenter.iastate.edu/2019/12/02address-at-davos-our-house-is-on-fire-jan-25-2019/.

79 "The Library of Life is burning": Gro Harlem Brundtland, "Speech at the United Nations Conference on Environment and Development (UNCED)," Rio de Janeiro, June 4, 1992,

transcript, https://www.un.org/en/conferences/environment/rio1992.

79 "the Tree of Life burning": "Völuspá," in Carolyne Larrington, trans., *The Poetic Edda* (Oxford: Oxford University Press, 1999), stanzas 47–48.

81 "Build a golden . . . to retreat across.": Robert Greene, *The 48 Laws of Power* (New York: Penguin Books, 1998), 181.

84–85 "This is the . . . and Mother Theresa.": Malala Yousafzai, *I Am Malala: The Girl Who Stood Up for Education and Was Shot by the Taliban* (New York: Little, Brown, 2013), 143.

85–86 "Thousands of people . . . can be heard.": Yousafzai, 333.

86 "No one can . . . change the world.": Yousafzai, 333.

86 "One child, one . . . change the world.": Yousafzai, 337.

86 "There's not a . . . States of America.": Barack Obama, "Barack Obama's Keynote Address at the 2004 Democratic National Convention," PBS News, July 27, 2004, transcript, https://www.pbs.org/newshour/show/barack-obamas-keynote-address-at-the-2004-democratic-national-convention.

87 "I can no . . . that I love.": Barack Obama, "Barack Obama's Speech on Race," *New York Times*, March 18, 2008, transcript, https://www.nytimes.com/2008/03/18/us/politics/18text-obama.html.

88 "It was remarkable . . . around the world.": Barack Obama quoted in Susan Ryan, "Obama Speaks in Dublin: 'Never Has a Nation So Small Inspired So Much in Another,'" Journal, May 23, 2011, https://www.thejournal.ie/obama-never-has-a-nation-so-small-inspired-so-much-in-another-142279-May2011/.

89–90 "For those of . . . rather difficult times.": Robert F. Kennedy, "Statement on the Assassination of Martin Luther King Jr., Indianapolis, Indiana, April 4, 1968," John F. Kennedy

Presidential Library and Museum, April 4, 1968, transcript, https://www.jfklibrary.org/learn/about-jfk/the-kennedy-family/robert-f-kennedy/robert-f-kennedy-speeches/statement-on-assassination-of-martin-luther-king-jr-indianapolis-indiana-april-4-1968.

93 "Wherever possible it . . . they deeply love.": Al Gore quoted in Charlie Melcher, host, "Episode 36: Talking to Al Gore About Climate Communication," *Future of StoryTelling*, podcast, April 2021, https://podcasts.apple.com/us/podcast/al-gore/id1501861146?i=1000518182418.

96 "When I have . . . Aha-moment for others.": Gore.

97–98 "In the spring . . . it did not.": Rune Kier Nielsen, "A Call to Democracy for Climate," *Vital Speeches International* 14, no. 1 (January 2022): 16–17.

98 "We must promise . . . That democracy works.": Nielsen.

100 "If I am . . . not now, when?": Hillel the Elder quoted in Marshall Ganz, *What Is Public Narrative: Self, Us & Now* (Public Narrative Worksheet—Working Paper, 2009), https://leadingchangenetwork.org/resource_center/what-is-public-narrative-self-us-and-now-public-narrative-worksheet-working-paper/.

104–105 "Tonight is a . . . me with pride.": Obama, "Barack Obama's Keynote Address."

112 "During my lifetime . . . prepared to die.": Nelson Mandela, "An Ideal for Which I Am Prepared to Die—Part 1," April 22, 2017, in Pretoria, South Africa, *Guardian* (US edition), transcript, https://www.theguardian.com/world/2007/apr/23/nelsonmandela1.

115 "I believe that . . . cause for disagreement.": Carsten Lyngdrup Madsen, *Nordboernes gamle religion* (Copenhagen: Univers, 2016), translated by the author, 516–517.

115–116 "The start of . . . must be destroyed.": Madsen, 516–517.

117 "nudging . . . that is . . . not rational choices.": Richard H. Thaler and Cass R. Sunstein, *Nudge: Improving Decisions About Health, Wealth, and Happiness* (New Haven, CT: Yale University Press, 2008), 6.

122 "I have a dream," Martin Luther King Jr. quoted in Gary Younge, *The Speech—The Story Behind Martin Luther King Jr.'s Dream* (Chicago: Guardian Books, 2013), 93.

122–123 "a great beacon . . . of justice emerges.": King quoted in Younge, 10.

124 "Tell them about the dream, Martin!": Mahalia Jackson quoted in Younge, 163–165.

124 "the table of . . . whirlwind of hate.": King quoted in Younge, 158.

125 "For we must . . . are upon us.": John Winthrop, "A Model of Christian Charity," speech delivered aboard the *Arabella*, 1630, in Charles S. Hyneman and Donald S. Lutz, eds., *American Political Writing During the Founding Era 1760–1805* (Indianapolis: Liberty Fund, 1983), 22.

126 "So that if . . . through the world.": Winthrop, 22.

126 "But if our . . . to possess it.": Winthrop, 22.

128 "we shall fight on the beaches": Winston S. Churchill, "We Shall Fight on the Beaches," speech delivered to the House of Commons, June 4, 1940, in Winston S. Churchill, *Winston S. Churchill: His Complete Speeches 1897–1963*, vol. 2, ed. Robert Rhodes James (New York: Chelsea House, 1974), 1616.

128 "band of brothers": Winston S. Churchill, "We Shall Not Fail," speech delivered to the House of Commons, June 18, 1940, in Winston S. Churchill, *The Second World War: Their Finest Hour* (London: Cassell, 1957), 115.

128 "their finest hour": Churchill, 129.

129 "we shall fight . . . shall never surrender.": Winston Churchill, "We Shall Fight on the Beaches," June 4, 1940, in London, International Churchill Society, transcript, https://winstonchurchill.org/resources/speeches/1940-the-finest-hour/we-shall-fight-on-the-beaches/.

130 "Ask not what . . . for your country.": John F. Kennedy, "Inaugural Address," January 20, 1961, in *Public Papers of the Presidents of the United States: John F. Kennedy, 1961*, ed. James W. Silver (Washington, DC: U.S. Government Printing Office, 1962), 2.

130 "The one unchangeable . . . unchangeable or certain.": John F. Kennedy, "Address at the United Nations," September 25, 1961, in Kennedy, 115.

130 "Let us never . . . fear to negotiate.": John F. Kennedy, "Inaugural Address," January 20, 1961, in Kennedy, 18.

130 "Don't let it . . . be another Camelot.": Jacqueline Kennedy quoted in Theodore H. White, *A Tour of the White House with Mrs. John F. Kennedy* (New York: Harcourt Brace Jovanovich, 1962), 37.

131 "Metaphors are the . . . weapon of communication": Simon Lancaster, *You Are Not Human: How Words Kill* (London: Biteback, 2019), 61.

131 "The library of . . . of the books.": Gro Harlem Brundtland, "Speech at the World Summit on Sustainable Development," Johannesburg, South Africa, September 2, 2002, in *Global Public Goods and Sustainable Development: A World Summit Reader*, ed. John Smith (London: Earthscan, 2003), 15.

132–133 "Gro Harlem Brundtland . . . with each other.": Kirsten Brosbøl, "The Burning Issue of Biodiversity," *Vital Speeches International* 7, no. 4 (April 2015): 112–113.

139 "I observe, gentlemen . . . belong to you.": Alexander the Great quoted in Arrian, *The Campaigns of Alexander*, trans. E. J. Chinnock (London: Heinemann, 1929), 237.

143 "I could not . . . those who return.": Alexander the Great quoted in Arrian, 238.

145 "have shared the . . . for your taking": Alexander the Great quoted in Arrian, 238.

145 "The conquered territory . . . into your hands.": Alexander the Great quoted in Arrian, 236.

149 "the particular . . . the universal": Chaïm Perelman and Lucie Olbrechts-Tyteca, *The New Rhetoric: A Treatise on Argumentation*, trans. John Wilkinson and Purcell W. Coleman (Notre Dame, IN: University of Notre Dame Press, 1969), 28–29.

166 "The first is . . . from the heavens.": "Völuspá," in Jean I. Young, trans. *The Poetic Edda* (New York: American-Scandinavian Foundation, 1932), 19.

168 "His hair was . . . land and town.": Hans Christian Andersen, "Agnete and the Merman," in Maria Krøyer, trans. *Danish Fairy Tales and Folklore* (Copenhagen: Gyldendal, 2020), 48.

169 "Think of the . . . across all land!": Andersen, 50.

# SELECTED BIBLIOGRAPHY

Aristotle. *Rhetoric.* Translated by W. Rhys Roberts. New York: Dover, 2004. First published in ca. 350 BCE.

Attenborough, David. *The Green Planet: Protecting Our Planet's Future.* London: BBC Books, 2023.

———. *A Life on Our Planet: My Witness Statement and a Vision for the Future.* London: BBC Books, 2020.

Cekic, Özlem. *Overcoming Hate Through Dialogue: Confronting Prejudice, Racism, and Bigotry with Conversation—and Coffee.* Miami: Mango, 2020.

Dixson-Declève, Sandrine, Owen Gaffney, and Jayati Ghosh. *Earth for All: A Survival Guide for Humanity.* Gabriola Island, BC: New Society, 2022.

Duarte, Nancy. *Resonate: Present Visual Stories That Transform Audiences.* Rev. ed. New York: Wiley, 2020.

Eriksson, Anne. *Urgent Message from a Hot Planet: How to Communicate Climate Change and Adapt to the Future.* London: Green Books, 2021.

Figueres, Christiana, and Tom Rivett-Carnac. *The Future We Choose: Surviving the Climate Crisis.* New York: Alfred A. Knopf, 2020.

Gallo, Carmine. *Talk Like TED: The 9 Public-Speaking Secrets of the World's Top Minds.* Rev. ed. New York: St. Martin's, 2021.

Ganz, Marshall. *What Is Public Narrative: Self, Us & Now* (Public Narrative Worksheet—Working Paper, 2009). https://leadingchangenetwork.org/resource_center/what-is-public-narrative-self-us-and-now-public-narrative-worksheet-working-paper/.

Gore, Al. *Earth in the Balance: Ecology and the Human Spirit.* Emmaus, PA: Henry Holt, 1992.

———. *An Inconvenient Truth: The Planetary Emergency of Global Warming and What We Can Do About It*. Emmaus, PA: Henry Holt, 2006.

Hayhoe, Katharine. *Saving Us: A Climate Scientist's Case for Hope and Healing in a Divided World*. New York: One Signal, 2021.

Hernandez, Isaias. *How to Save Our Planet: The Facts, the Science, and the Solutions*. New York: Penguin Books, 2022.

Hogan, Clover. *It's Not a Climate Crisis, It's a Climate Emergency: How to Transform Our World*. London: Templar, 2021.

Huntley, Rebecca. *How to Talk About Climate Change in a Way That Makes a Difference*. Melbourne: Scribe, 2020.

Jaquette, Sarah. *Field Guide to Climate Anxiety: How to Keep Your Cool on a Warming Planet*. New York: Hachette Books, 2023.

Kennedy, John F. *Selected Speeches*. Edited by David Talbot. New York: Little, Brown, 1997.

Lancaster, Simon. *You Are Not Human: How Words Kill*. London: Biteback, 2019.

———. *Winning Minds: Secrets from the Language of Leadership*. New York: Palgrave Macmillan, 2015.

Loach, Mikaela. *It's Not That Radical: Climate Action to Transform Our World*. London: DK, 2023.

Luntz, Frank. *Words That Work: It's Not What You Say, It's What People Hear*. New York: Hyperion, 2007.

Macy, Joanna, and Chris Johnstone. *Active Hope: How to Face the Mess We're in Without Going Crazy*. Novato, CA: New World Library, 2012.

Mandela, Nelson. *Long Walk to Freedom: The Autobiography of Nelson Mandela*. New York: Little, Brown, 1994.

McKibben, Bill. *Eaarth: Making a Life on a Tough New Planet.* New York: Henry Holt, 2010.

———. *Falter: Has the Human Game Begun to Play Itself Out?* New York: Henry Holt, 2019.

Meacham, Jon. *And There Was Light: Abraham Lincoln and the American Struggle.* New York: Random House, 2022.

Perelman, Chaïm, and Lucie Olbrechts-Tyteca. *The New Rhetoric: A Treatise on Argumentation.* Translated by John Wilkinson and Purcell W. Coleman. Notre Dame, IN: University of Notre Dame Press, 1969.

Phillips, Ben. *How to Fight Inequality: (and Why That Fight Needs You).* Hoboken, NJ: John Wiley & Sons, 2020.

Robinson, Mary. *Climate Justice: Hope, Resilience, and the Fight for a Sustainable Future.* London: Bloomsbury, 2018.

Thomas, Leah. *The Intersectional Environmentalist: How to Dismantle Systems of Oppression to Protect People + Planet.* New York: HarperOne, 2022.

Thunberg, Greta. *The Climate Book: The Facts and the Solutions.* London: Penguin, 2023.

———. *No One Is Too Small to Make a Difference.* London: Penguin, 2019.

Toye, Richard. *The Roar of the Lion: Nine Great Speeches That Changed the World.* London: Oxford University Press, 2019.

Younge, Gary. *The Speech: The Story Behind Martin Luther King Jr.'s Dream.* Chicago: Guardian Books, 2013.

Yousafzai, Malala. *I Am Malala: The Girl Who Stood Up for Education and Was Shot by the Taliban.* New York: Little, Brown, 2013.

# FURTHER INFORMATION

## Speeches

Cekic, Özlem. "Why I Have Coffee with People Who Send Me Hate Mail." TED talk, New York, September 2018. 15:11. https://www.ted.com/talks/ozlem_cekic_why_i_have_coffee_with_people_who_send_me_hate_mail?subtitle=en.
Özlem Cekic advocates for engaging with those who disagree with you to foster understanding and dialogue, especially on polarizing issues.

Espen Stoknes, Per. "How to Transform Apocalypse Fatigue into Action on Global Warming." TED talk, New York, September 2017. 14:50. https://www.ted.com/talks/per_espen_stoknes_how_to_transform_apocalypse_fatigue_into_action_on_global_warming?subtitle=en.
Per Espen Stoknes explores how to overcome the psychological barriers to climate action and motivate people to engage with the issue.

Gore, Al. "What the Fossil Fuel Industry Doesn't Want You to Know." TED talk, Detroit, July 2023. 25:44. https://www.ted.com/talks/al_gore_what_the_fossil_fuel_industry_doesn_t_want_you_to_know?referrer=playlist-countdown_session_1_urgency&subtitle=en.
Al Gore reveals the tactics used by the fossil fuel industry to undermine climate science and delay action.

Hayhoe, Katharine. "The Most Important Thing You Can Do to Fight Climate Change: Talk About It." TED talk, Palm Springs, CA, November 2018. 17:02. https://www.ted.com/talks/katharine_hayhoe_the_most_important_thing_you_can_do_to_fight_climate_change_talk_about_it?subtitle=en.
Katharine Hayhoe emphasizes the importance of climate conversations in building collective will to address the climate crisis.

Hogan, Clover. "What to Do When Climate Feels Unstoppable."

TED talk, London, February 2021. 12:24. https://www.ted.com/talks/clover_hogan_what_to_do_when_climate_change_feels_unstoppable?subtitle=en.
Clover Hogan offers strategies for young people feeling overwhelmed by the climate crisis, focusing on empowerment and activism.

Neubauer, Luisa. "Why You Should Be a Climate Activist." TED talk, München, Germany, July 2019. 17:34. https://www.ted.com/talks/luisa_neubauer_why_you_should_be_a_climate_activist?subtitle=en.
Luisa Neubauer, one of the leaders of Fridays for Future, explains the power of activism in driving climate action.

Rasmussen, Rune Hjarnø. "How Attaching Kinship to Land Can Help Biodiversity | Rune Hjarnø Rasmussen | TEDxTralee." TEDx Talks, Tralee, Ireland, posted November 12, 2024. YouTube video. 14:31. https://www.youtube.com/watch?v=0R-2Cj3Kous.
Rasmussen talks about how we can use kinship to help solve the biodiversity crisis by learning from the animist knowledge of our ancestors.

Thunberg, Greta. "The Disarming Case to Act Right Now on Climate Change." TED talk, Stockholm, November 2018. 11:02. https://www.ted.com/talks/greta_thunberg_the_disarming_case_to_act_right_now_on_climate_change?subtitle=en.
Greta Thunberg calls for immediate and drastic action to combat climate change, urging everyone to take the crisis seriously.

Yousafzai, Malala. "Activism, Changemakers and Hope for the Future." TED talk, July 2020. 49:27. https://www.ted.com/talks/malala_yousafzai_activism_changemakers_and_hope_for_the_future?subtitle=en.
Malala Yousafzai discusses the role of young activists in shaping a more just and sustainable world, with a focus on girls' right to an education.

# Websites

Climate Central
https://www.climatecentral.org/
Climate Central is a research organization focused on climate science, impacts, and communication, providing information to help the public understand and respond to climate change.

Climate Communications Hub
https://climatecommshub.com/
The Climate Communications Hub works to enhance climate communication strategies, helping organizations to effectively engage with their audiences on climate issues.

Climate Outreach
https://climateoutreach.org/
Climate Outreach is a nonprofit organization dedicated to helping people communicate about climate change more effectively, bridging gaps between different communities and perspectives.

Count Us In
https://count-us-in.com/
Count Us In is a global initiative encouraging individuals to take steps to reduce their carbon footprint and influence leaders to act on climate change.

Fridays for Future US
https://fridaysforfutureusa.org/
Fridays for Future US is the United States chapter of a is a global youth-led movement inspired by Greta Thunberg, focused on climate strikes and demanding urgent action from governments to address the climate crisis.

Friends of the Earth
https://foe.org/
Friends of the Earth is an international network of environmental organizations advocating for a sustainable and just world through grassroots activism and policy change.

Greenpeace
https://www.greenpeace.org/
Greenpeace is an independent global campaigning organization that promotes solutions to environmental issues and advocates for a green and peaceful future.

Intergovernmental Panel on Climate Change (IPCC)
https://www.ipcc.ch/
The IPCC is the United Nations body responsible for assessing the science related to climate change. Discover a wealth of information on all aspects of the climate emergency here, yet know that it is aimed at a climate-literate audience.

Leading Change Network
https://leadingchangenetwork.org/
The Leading Change Network connects organizers, educators, and researchers to build the capacity for community leadership in social and environmental movements.

More in Common
https://moreincommon.com/
More in Common is a research organization that explores what drives societal polarization and how to foster social cohesion and common ground in divided communities.

Neighbours United
https://neighboursunited.org/
Neighbours United empowers Canadian communities to address climate change at a local level, fostering collaboration and action among neighbors.

Nordic Animism
https://nordicanimism.com/
Nordic Animism is run by Rune Hjarnø Rasmussen and provides research and practices to renew previous ages' animist knowledge and cultural heritage to better understand and address the challenges of the climate crisis and the loss of biodiversity.

People's Climate Vote
https://peoplesclimate.vote/
The People's Climate Vote, the world's largest survey of public opinion on climate change, is conducted by the United Nations Development Programme. It is a great place to go to find the most recent global opinions—and they are often quite calming.

Talk Climate Change
https://talkclimatechange.org/
Talk Climate Change is an initiative aimed at fostering open and constructive dialogues about climate change to inspire action and awareness.

10 Billion Solutions
https://10billionsolutions.com/
10 Billion Solutions is an initiative aimed at addressing the global climate crisis through innovative solutions and collective action. The idea is to turn the threat of ten billion people in the future into an asset for climate action.

350.org
https://350.org/
Bill McKibben founded 350.org as a global climate grassroots organization delivering training and organizing around climate action.

United Nations: ACT NOW: Speak Up
https://www.unep.org/interactives/things-you-can-do-climate-emergency/

This campaign encourages individual actions to address the climate emergency, offering practical steps to reduce your carbon footprint and ways to use your voice to strengthen the case for climate action.

United Nations Foundation: Say It with Science
https://sayitwithscience.org/
The United Nations Foundation's "Say It with Science" initiative promotes evidence-based communication about climate change to help people understand the science behind the crisis. It caters to people having a hard time understanding the IPCC.

We Don't Have Time
https://wedonthavetime.org/
We Don't Have Time is a social media platform for climate action, where users can share ideas, influence decision-makers, and support sustainable solutions.

World Speech Day
https://worldspeechday.com/
A collection of impactful speeches delivered globally. This platform highlights speeches from different events and occasions, showcasing a diverse array of voices.

Yale Climate Change Communication
https://climatecommunication.yale.edu/
Yale Climate Change Communication conducts research on public knowledge and attitudes about climate change and provides resources to improve climate change communication.

Youth at UNFCCC Conferences
https://unfccc.int/topics/education-and-youth/youth/youth-engagement/youth-for-climate-action-youth-unfccc-conferences Explore what young people across the globe are doing to fight climate change, and read lists of youth activities and events at UN Climate Change Conferences.

# Podcasts

"Behavior and Communication, Episode 2": *Rethink Climate*
https://www.bbc.co.uk/programmes/m001gkq8
The host of *Rethink Climate*, Amol Rajan, talks to Tom Bailey, Meghan Kennedy-Woodard, and George Marshall about the psychological aspects of climate communication.

"Changing Minds Part 5: Getting Emotional": *In Over My Head*
https://www.inovermyheadpodcast.com/episodes/changing-minds-part-5
In this episode of *In Over My Head*, Michael Bartz hosts University of Groningen's Linda Steg, who speaks about the connection between emotion and pro-environmental behavior.

*Climate Curious*
https://tedxlondon.com/podcast/
*Climate Curious*, hosted by Maryam Pasha and Ben Hurst, explores the various facets of the climate crisis, featuring diverse voices and stories to inspire listeners to take action.

*Climate Now*
https://climatenow.com/podcast/
*Climate Now*, hosted by James Lawler, delves into the science, policy, and economics of climate change, featuring experts who discuss current challenges and potential solutions.

*Communicating Climate Change*
https://communicatingclimatechange.com/podcast
This podcast by Climate Outreach and hosted by Dickon Bonvik-Stone focuses on how to effectively communicate climate change to diverse audiences, featuring insights from experts in the field.

"Episode 132: Interview with Professor Katharine Hayhoe on How to Have a Conversation on the Highly Politicized and Divisive Subject of Climate Change": *The Sustainability Agenda*

https://share.transistor.fm/s/def67601
Fergal Byrne hosts Katharine Hayhoe, who describes why we need to talk about climate change and how to create collective action.

*The Friendly Ghost*
https://friendlyghost.buzzsprout.com/
*The Friendly Ghost*, hosted by Felicity Barber, is mainly about speechwriting and public speaking, offering tips and insights on how to communicate effectively in various settings.

*Future of StoryTelling*
https://futureofstorytelling.org/work/podcasts/
Charlie Melcher hosts this podcast, which explores how storytelling can be used to drive social change, including episodes focused on climate change narratives.

*Outrage + Optimism*
https://www.outrageandoptimism.org/
This podcast explores climate solutions with a blend of outrage at the scale of the challenge and optimism about our capacity to address it. Christiana Figueres, Tom Rivett-Carnac, and Paul Dickinson are the hosts.

*Planet Possible*
https://planetpossible.eco/
*Planet Possible*, hosted by Niki Roach, highlights innovative solutions to the environmental challenges facing our planet, featuring stories from around the world.

# INDEX

Age of Enlightenment, 26–30
"Agnete and the Merman," 168–170
Alexander the Great, 13–14
  speeches of, 139–146
anaphora, 7
Aristotle, 11–12, 27, 30
  *See also* rhetoric
Arthur, King, 38
Attenborough, David, 41–43

Biden, Joe, 22–23, 42–43, 52–55, 76–78
biodiversity, 10, 42–43, 62, 131–132
Brundtland, Gro Harlem, 17–19, 79, 131–132

carbon dioxide ($CO_2$), 17, 30
chlorofluorocarbon (CFC) gases, 64–68
Cicero, Marcus Tullius, 15–16
Civil Rights Movement, 71–73
climate as security, 53–55
climate communication, 91, 102.
  history of, 16–17
  word choice for, 43–44, 56
  *See also* Luntz, Frank
Climate COP, 19, 22, 41, 96, 98
climate denial tactics, 48–50
climate silence, 157–158
Columbus, Christopher, 72–73
community building in speech, 108–110, 113, 142, 152, 155
creating commitment in speech, 107–119
Cullis-Suzuki, Severn, 19–20

Democratic National Convention, 54–55, 86

Dialogue Coffee, 82–84
dominant narrative, 109–110
doubt, 48–52, 95–96

Earth Summit, 18–21
emotional brain, 141–143
empathy, 90, 138–139

fear of public speaking, 25
Fimbul Winter, 164–167, 170–171
framing, 26, 43–59
Francis (pope), 41–42

Ganz, Marshall, 70, 99–100, 103–104
Gates, Bill, 134
golden bridge, 81–93
  definition of, 81–82
Gore, Al, 21, 45
  interviews of, 93
  publications of, 21, 78
Guterres, António, 23, 56–58

Harris, Kamala, 53–55
herd mentality, 117–119, 156
Hogan, Clover, 62–63

*Inconvenient Truth, An. See* Gore, Al
instinctive brain, 137–141
Intergovernmental Panel on Climate Change (IPCC), 21–22, 49

Kennedy, John F., 124–125, 130, 151
Kennedy, Robert F., 88–89
King, Martin Luther, Jr., 88–90
  speeches of, 122–124, 126, 149
Kyoto Procotol, 19–20, 45

Lakoff, George, 43–44, 55, 58–59
Lancaster, Simon, 131, 137–138
logical brain, 143–147
Luntz, Frank, 45–52, 58
 climate denial, 48–50

Mandela, Nelson, 110–113
Merlin, 38–39
metaphor, 14–16, 50–52, 55–59,
 103–105, 125–127, 131–133,
 138–141
 common metaphors, 56–57,
 76–78, 125
 criticism of, 57–58, 76–77
 definition of, 14–15
Montreal Protocol, 68–69

*New Rhetoric: A Treatise on
 Argumentation, The*, 149
Nixon, Richard, 88, 151

Obama, Barack, 21, 48, 150–151
 speeches of, 86–88, 103–105,
 146–147, 153–154
One Ring method, 127–135
*Our Common Future* (Bruntland
 Report), 17–18
ozone layer, 63–69

Paris Agreement. *See* Climate COP
pause in speech, 145–147
public narrative, 99–103
 story of now, 101–103
 story of self, 100
 story of us, 100–101

quilombos, 72–76

Ragnarok, 164–167, 170.
 *See also* Fimbul Winter

Reagan, Ronald, 17, 125
Republican National Convention,
 54
rhetoric, 137–147
Roosevelt, Franklin D., 76, 131,
 150–151
rule of three, 144–145

sense of community, 108–110,
 113, 152, 155
*Soul City*, 107–108
speaking online, 151–156
State of the Union address, 47,
 108, 151, 153–154

TED talks, 133–135, 153,
 155–157
Thatcher, Margaret, 17–18
Þorkelsson, Þorgeir, 113–117
Thunberg, Greta
 climate action of, 50
 speeches of, 31–32, 50, 52, 55,
 79, 130–132
tricolon. *See* rule of three
Trump, Donald, 22, 48, 50, 52,
 54, 76–77, 150

United Nations, 17–18, 23, 55,
 67–68, 84–85, 111–113,
 130–132
United Nations Framework
 Convention on Climate
 Change (UNFCCC), 18–19

Walz, Tim, 55
World War II, 11, 71, 78, 128, 150

Yousafzai, Malala, 36–37, 84–86

Zumbi (Francisco), 75–76

# ACKNOWLEDGMENTS

I want to start by offering my deep gratitude to all the people working for climate action every day—whether professionally, privately, or in any other way. You are my inspiration, and this book is my modest support for that grand endeavor of creating a better future than what we are looking into now.

I am also grateful to all the people who have provided insights for the research and comments on the process. Friends and colleagues across rhetoric, climate activism, and speechwriting: Thank you!

Finally, my agent Natalie Kimber, who saw a potential through the blurred prism of a Danish language manuscript, and my editors at Lerner Publishing for meticulously shaping it to be the best that it could be. Your belief in this book and your tireless work have meant the world.

# ABOUT THE AUTHOR

Rune Kier Nielsen has a master's degree in cultural anthropology focusing on mobilization for social movements and communication for social change. He is an acclaimed political speechwriter and communicator having worked for mayors in the Danish Capital of Copenhagen, the Danish government, and the United Nations Environment Programme. He has won Cicero Speechwriting Awards in two categories: Government and Environment/Energy/Sustainability. His speeches have been featured in the prominent magazine *Vital Speeches International* seven times. He has been a TEDx speaker coach and highlighted adviser for the World Speech Day, as well as a guest lecturer teaching climate communication and speechwriting at various universities and international conferences. He is a climate activist himself.

The views and opinions expressed in this book are those of the author and do not necessarily reflect the official policy or position of the UN, the Danish government, or any affiliated organizations.

# PHOTO ACKNOWLEDGMENTS

Image credits: Hans Blossey/Alamy, p. 12; Peter Hermes Furian/Alamy, p. 14; MARK CARDWELL/AFP/Getty Images, p. 18; Michael Wheatley/Alamy, p. 20; GeorgiosArt/Getty Images, p. 27; Johannes EISELE/AFP/Getty Images, p. 32; Nature Picture Library/Alamy, p. 34; PA Images/Alamy, p. 37; Danita Delimont/Alamy, p. 42; Michael Macor/The San Francisco Chronicle /Getty Images, p. 44; ANDREW CABALLERO-REYNOLDS/POOL/AFP / Getty Images, p. 46; Hollie Adams/Bloomberg/Getty Images, p. 52; UN Photo/Eskinder Debebe, p. 57; JULIEN DE ROSA/AFP/Getty Images, p. 62; NASA/Aura > OMI, p. 67; Allison Sales/picture alliance/Getty Images, p. 74; Carolyn Cole/Los Angeles Times/Getty Images, p. 77; Steen Thomassen/Wikimedia Commons (CC BY 3.0), p. 83; STAN HONDA/AFP/Getty Images, p. 85; AP Photo/Leroy Patton, Indianapolis News, p. 89; Gehad Hamdy/picture alliance/Getty Images, p. 96; Wikimedia Commons PD, pp. 99, 150; Brett Monroe Garner/Getty Images, p. 102; ALEXANDER JOE/AFP/Getty Images, p. 113; CNP/Getty Images, p. 123; mikroman6/Getty Images, p. 125; BelozerArt/Shutterstock, p. 128; MIGUEL MEDINA/AFP /Getty Images, p. 132; Heritage Image Partnership Ltd/Alamy, pp. 140, 164; Joe Raedle/Getty Images/Getty Images, p. 146; Courtesy of the author, p. 157; Miguel Medina/AFP/Getty Images, 158; Charles Walker Collection/Alamy, p. 164; Russell Mountford/Alamy, p. 169.

Cover: boromvit tatasai/Shutterstock; LuibovK/Shutterstock; maxim ibragimov/Shutterstock;lovelyday12/Shutterstock; helgafo/Shutterstock; chen xue bing/Shutterstock; ids design/Shutterstock; 4clover/Shutterstock.